REAL ESTATE
DEBT CAN MAKE
YOU RICH

REAL ESTATE
DEBT CAN MAKE
YOU RICH

STEVE DEXTER

McGraw-Hill

New York   Chicago   San Francisco   Lisbon   London
Madrid   Mexico City   Milan   New Delhi   San Juan
Seoul   Singapore   Sydney   Toronto

1 2 3 4 5 6 7 8 9 0 DOC/DOC 0 9 8 7 6

ISBN-13: 978-0-07-147281-4
ISBN-10:   0-07-147281-9

McGraw-Hill books are available at special quantity discounts to use as premiums and sales promotions, or for use in corporate training programs. For more information, please write to the Director of Special Sales, McGraw-Hill Professional, Two Penn Plaza, New York, NY 10121-2298. Or contact your local bookstore.

The eternal spirit of my journalist father, John W. Dexter, was always with me while I was carving out the words for this book, because the ink that ran in his veins runs in mine, too. The heritage of writing for the public has come full circle.

CONTENTS

FOREWORD

I have known Steve Dexter for about 10 years and have watched him develop from an excellent mortgage broker into a highly popular instructor at many Southern California community colleges, then into one of our financial mentors, and now into a very successful author.

Steve is a first-rate real estate investor whose financial advice has always been exceptional and on the cutting edge. I believe this book will become the bible of real estate financing, and I am very proud to have been his mentor and friend. I believe that all those who read his book will never finance their properties the old way again.

Dr. Marshall E. Reddick, Ph.D.
Retired Professor of Economics
California State University—Los Angeles

ACKNOWLEDGMENTS

I am especially grateful to Mary Glenn, acquisitions editor at McGraw-Hill, for giving me a chance to make my views known.

Sincere thanks also go out to all the mentors and coaches who have blazed the sometimes treacherous trails of real estate investing before me. I want to acknowledge my friend Dr. Marshall Reddick for generously offering his free help and also Jack Miller for giving me his time-proven wisdom.

I am deeply grateful for the insight of Dr. David Schumacher and his wife, Margaret, whose advice made this book better than it would have been otherwise. Dr. Schumacher is the author of *Buy and Hold— 7 Steps to a Real Estate Fortune,* which is the bible for long-term real estate investing. His insight taught me that the inherent value of holding property in quality neighborhoods will build wealth. I am saddened to learn of his recent passing. He was a giant of a man and will be sorely missed by all those who benefitted from his astute comments and enormous generosity.

Thanks to John Schaub, whose clear teachings have made the road to real estate wealth more certain and less scary. I thank Pete Fortunato, whose teachings showed me how to negotiate and creatively structure real estate deals. I cannot forget Jack Fullerton, whose craggy input was always welcome—although not at first. I would be remiss if I did not mention Mic Blackwell, whose timeworn street knowledge helped me from making too many mistakes. My thanks also go to Mike Cantu, one of the best negotiators and savvy wholesale house buyers I know.

A special thanks goes to Bob Bruss, who thought my writing was good enough for public consumption. Bob Bruss writes for the national media, and I have always enjoyed his articles.

Finally, I am grateful to my loving wife, Susan, whose unwavering support has made me the man I am today. There is no substitute for having a close spouse who is there every step of the way and off whom I can bounce my crazy ideas. Thank you for being there, and I love you a lot.

INTRODUCTION: WHY GOOD REAL ESTATE FINANCING IS ESSENTIAL TO YOUR FINANCIAL HEALTH

I t is amazing to look at the distribution of wealth today. In the United States, almost 70 percent of all households own their own homes, and it is estimated that the vast majority of the average American's wealth is tied up in his or her home. In the *Millionaire Next Door,* a best-selling study profiling the average American millionaire, Thomas Stanley found that most wealthy households own their own houses and at least one other investment property.

Yet the other 30 percent of American households, either by choice or by circumstance, are in danger of never owning their own homes and certainly no investment property. This disturbing trend between the "haves" and the "have nots" is the difference between those who own property and those who do not.

Never before has there been such a huge variety of loan programs, making the dream of homeownership here in the United States more possible than anywhere else on the world or at any time in history.

Why does the United States have more millionaires than any other country? Why are we the light of the world—a beacon of hope for all those dreaming of homeownership? The answer is threefold:

1. The average consumer has easy access to sophisticated financial markets where many loan products are created.
2. In this country we hold private-property rights to be most sacred. The American system of justice respects property rights.
3. The average American homeowner knows that his or her home is not going to be molested by a powerful government or somebody with more money.

Really? Our property rights are unmolested? You might think our property rights are being threatened because of recent liberal use of eminent-domain laws. The U.S. Supreme Court made a very unpopular decision it its *Kelo v. New London* ruling, where the city of New London was allowed to take over private property. The public outcry from the perception that the city had misused eminent domain to force out homeowners and small businesses that stood in the way of commercial development has produced much discussion and pending legislation. But nobody really knows the long-term effect.

THE POWER OF LEVERAGING AND OF GREAT FINANCING

Using other people's money (OPM) allows you to leverage your property. You get to put the bank's money to work for you. If you buy a $200,000 house for all cash and it appreciates 10 percent, or $20,000, you have an asset that is worth $220,000. Your return on investment, or yield, is just 10 percent.

Instead, say that you bought the house for 10 percent ($20,000) down, and the other 90 percent ($180,000) was good bank financing. This is what is called *90 percent loan to value* (LTV). The bank loaned you $180,000 of its money because you are young, beautiful, and successful. Since you are so smart, you realize that because your house has gone up in value $20,000, you have made a return of 100 percent instead of 10 percent.

So what do you want—a 10 percent or a 100 percent yield on your investment?

EVERYTHING YOU NEED TO KNOW ABOUT REAL ESTATE FINANCE

WHAT YOU OWE TODAY IS WHAT YOU WILL BE WORTH TOMORROW

Does the idea of being millions of dollars in debt scare you? It shouldn't. As long as that debt is attached to a house in a good area, you will have the awesome power of leveraging working for you. In Part 2 we will talk extensively about how to find houses in superior areas so that you can put that astounding power of using the bank's money to work for you.

Most people pay their credit cards, car loans, and living expenses with after-tax money. Unless you have a business reason for writing it off, you cannot deduct credit card interest or car expenses. After Uncle Sam has taken his fair share, you are trying to live on the rest. Then you pay for your living expenses.

You need mortgage debt, not consumer debt.

TAX SAVINGS

Interest on mortgage debt and property taxes for your primary residence are tax deductible on Schedule A of your federal tax return. This reduces the cost of owning your home. By being able to itemize your deductions, you liberate other deductions. Your itemized deductions can include:

1. Charitable contributions and gifts (cash, cars, furniture)
2. Real estate taxes paid on your residence
3. Personal property taxes
4. Sales taxes on everything you bought during the year
5. Casualty and theft losses
6. State and local income taxes
7. Unreimbursed employee expenses
8. Medical expenses and some business expenses
9. Job-change expenses
10. Tax preparation fees
11. Union dues

Check with your tax professional because some restrictions may apply.

I am in the 34.3 percent tax bracket (25 percent federal and 9.3 percent State of California). Thus I only really pay 34.3 percent of the interest the bank charges me. If my mortgage on a house is 6 percent, my after-tax interest rate is only 3.94 percent. The government pays the rest. And you also get to deduct your property taxes for your primary residence. The same applies for second homes not used as investment property, although there have been rumblings on Capitol Hill about changing the second-home deduction as Congress grapples with mounting budget deficits.

Only when you itemize are you able to escape the limited standard deduction. In 2006, the standard deduction is $10,300 for married taxpayers filing jointly and $5,150 for single taxpayers. It is not hard to surpass those low limits. According to Section 121 of the tax code, when you sell your principal residence, any capital gain is tax-free up to $250,000 for individuals and $500,000 for married couples.

TAX ADVANTAGES OF OWNING INVESTMENT PROPERTY ARE FABULOUS

With investment property (property held out for rental), you can deduct your mortgage interest, property taxes, insurance, depreciation, and anything else having to do with the upkeep and management of the property.

As long as you materially participate in running your soon-to-be real estate empire, other tax deductions can include:

1. Auto expenses
2. Airline travel, hotels, and restaurants when you travel to your property
3. Educational seminars, tapes, Internet costs, magazine/news-letter subscriptions, and books (such as the book you have in your hand)
4. Office expenses to manage your real estate
5. Depreciation—The Internal Revenue Service (IRS) says that your building (not the land value) has a useful life of 27.5 years, so you get to deduct 1/27.5 percent for 27.5 years.

Also, when you buy a house, the points (1 point is 1 percent of the loan amount) and prepaid interest are tax deductible in the year of purchase. Other closing costs can be added to your basis in the property. Points paid for a refinance loan are deducted over the lifetime of the loan. If you refinance or pay off that loan early, you then can deduct those points the year of payoff. The same applies for any early payoff of prepayment penalties. Check with your tax professional for the exact numbers.

Therefore, you have two choices in life: You can either pay taxes or buy real estate. The IRS with these fantastic tax breaks, Wall Street where many of the various innovative loan products are created, and I who wrote this book all want you to own real estate.

THE STATE OF THE MORTGAGE MARKETS TODAY AND TOMORROW

Ease of Money and the Vast Array of Loan Products Available

In recent years, lower interest rates and ease of credit have prevailed. In times of economic recession, governments and central banks are inclined toward accommodation—lowering the barrier for business startups and expansion. National central banks worldwide make it easier for businesses to borrow money by lowering the cost of borrowing. As the economic recovery gains strength, governments typically will tighten credit and circulate less money to curtail inflation. Currently, we have historically low interest rates that aid businesses and people wanting to buy homes.

Not only have low interest rates made it less costly to own real estate, but the explosion of mortgage products being sold on the secondary market is unprecedented. You have more choices than you ever have had to finance your home or investment property. I will cover the many types of loans later in this book.

But let's not get ahead of ourselves. What is a secondary market?

Secondary Markets

When I first started as a mortgage broker 15 years ago, there were many fewer choices in the types of loans available. Buyers had to put at least

5 percent down to buy a house and at least 20 percent down to purchase investment property, if they could find it. There were the garden-variety 30- and 15-year fixed-rate loans, as well as some 5- and 7-year balloon-payment loans (more on exactly what these loans are later). The major savings and loan institutions that had not gone belly up or been swallowed up by larger banks had adjustable-rate loans. A few places had subprime loans and hard-money loans at very high rates for consumers with bad credit. That was it.

Now, if you get a loan from a broker, a bank, a credit union, or another financial institution, you are getting it on the *primary market.* Unless the lending institution keeps the loan in its own portfolio, the loan will get sold on the *secondary market.* The loan will get packaged in a securitized bundle and then sold to an insurance company, pension fund, wealthy individual, or a fixed-income fund on Wall Street. The servicing rights can be separated while still another investor owns the mortgage. Other interest-only features of the loan can be stripped off and sold separately to become another type of security called a *derivative.* This is why your home loan gets bought and sold several times while you have it.

There is a huge appetite for these "bundled mortgages" backed by American real estate. These securities are called *collateralized mortgage obligations* (CMOs) and are almost as safe as U.S. Treasury bonds—the safest security in the world. And they pay a higher rate. This growing need for safe returns has caused the secondary market to be more aggressive and to come up with many new and different loan products.

The American home buyer has benefited from these innovations. Some of these new loans not seen before are:

- 100 percent financing for fourplexes, non-owner-occupied
- 5 percent down for non-owner-occupied properties for borrowers with bad credit
- 2-, 3-, 5-, and 30-year fixed-interest-only loans
- No documentation and stated income loans for people with impaired credit

Most of these loans can be had at fairly attractive rates. Speaking of interest rates, what causes these rates to go up and down?

Interest Rates—Nobody Knows Exactly Why and How the Market Will Move

If I could predict interest rates, I would be in the wrong business.

I get calls all the time from people who want to know where rates are going. I tell them that I just got my crystal ball out of the shop. It was broken, but the people who fixed it tell me it is working fine now. After 16 years of watching the movements in the bond market, I can tell you that anybody who claims that he or she can predict exactly where interest rates will be is lying. Economists and others who are supposed to be "in the know" have been predicting for years that long-term rates should be 1 to 2 percent higher than they are at present. They have been wrong.

Professional bond traders can't predict the market either. They are gamblers, just as in Vegas, and they lose money all the time.

I challenge you to make sense of the following commentary on the daily 10-year Treasury bond market from a market-tracking service I subscribe to.

> **10-Yr: +01/32 . . . 4.579 percent . . . GNMAs: +02/32 . . . USD/JPY: 117.7100 . . . EUR/USD: 1.1908**
>
> **Bond Market Churns in Quiet Trade:** Trade **meandered mixed** in the treasuries, with the long-end sitting under water while shorter-maturities pulled a touch better. The market was unenthused & much of the action was spreading. Players **continued to unwind flattener plays throughout the session**, tipping the yield curve in a very tight range, the **2–10-yr backed that yield spread up to –8.4 from an early –9.8** & the 2–30-yr yields were chased back to –11.4 from –13.8. The market eyed falling commodities, but event risk on deck is far too com-

pelling to elicit a reaction. The market will be looking out to the start of the week tomorrow (today did not seem to count for much) when **economic data starts hitting & new Federal Reserve nominees get grilled at their confirmation hearings.**

Understand this? I don't either, completely. I probably can tell you more how these remarks fit into the larger picture of economic trends. I can tell you what interest rates the economy favors long term and if the market is likely to be volatile because of a pending announcement. But I still get surprised every day.

You can, however, talk about the direction of the economy.

Where Will Interest Rates Be Next Month, Next Year, in Five Years?

They will go up—and down. Then they will go up again.

I hate to sound so flippant, but nobody can say for sure. It can get very complicated. It is more helpful to ask in what long-term direction the economy is headed. If the economy is coming out of a recession, rates generally rise to prevent runaway inflation. If the economy is headed toward a recession, rates usually trend downward. This lessens the cost of borrowed money so that businesses can do other things with their money, such as purchase capital equipment and hire more employees.

All along the way, there are many short-term gyrations. Rates will jump for a while and then recede. Sometimes I see a time when interest rates fall into a lull for a bit and then mysteriously pop upward. On one day when the Federal Reserve announced a ¼ point increase in the discount rate, mortgage rates actually *declined* ¼ percent.

All eyes are fixed on what the chairman of the Federal Reserve says when he conducts monetary policy. The Fed controls the short-term *federal funds rate,* which is the rate member banks charge each other, and the *overnight discount rate,* which is the rate member banks are charged for short-term borrowings directly from the Fed. When the chairman talks, all financial institutions wait with bated breath.

But first they have to decipher what Fed Chairman Alan Greenspan said in his July 19, 2004, testimony before the Senate Banking committee: "The considerable monetary accommodation put in place starting in 2001 is becoming increasingly unnecessary." *Translation*: The economy doesn't need interest rates to remain this low in order to prosper.

New Fed Chairman Ben Bernanke has promised to make his comments more understandable and his actions more transparent, but you can be sure that his performance is being watched by the bond traders. When the Fed speaks, the ears of the international financial markets are wide open.

Mortgage rates are driven by:

1. Bond traders'/investor's perception of the strength or weakness of the U.S economy
2. The supply of new debt coming on the market and how much demand there is for it
3. The inflationary stance of the Federal Reserve, the government's central bank

If you are wondering what kind of loan to get and you are keeping an eye on how mortgage rates will move in the future, I have some strategies for you. Later on in this book I will help you to choose the right loan based on where you think rates are going. And, in Part 2, I will talk a lot about what kind of house to get and in what kinds of neighborhoods to look.

Lenders Are Very Risk-Averse

Although I will cover in depth how lenders grade the property they lend on, I first want to give you a glimpse at how lenders think.

Lenders are very risk-adverse. The more risk there is for lenders, the more you will pay in higher interest rates and increased costs. Lenders have spent millions on computer programs that predict how likely it is that a particular borrower is going to default on his or her payments. Lenders *hate* getting foreclosed property back because they generally lose money. They are in the business of loaning money, not running foreclosure departments.

Banks loathe the prospect of getting a house back after a lengthy and sometimes ugly foreclosure. Every day without a payment being made is a day that a loan is nonperforming. There are many tricks people in foreclosure can employ to prolong the foreclosure proceedings and stay in the house. By the time the bank gets the house back, it has probably deteriorated in condition. I have seen some houses in horrible condition where the owner had taken a sledgehammer to the walls, stolen all the toilets, and left live electrical wires hanging from the ceilings. In one, when the disgruntled former owner was finally evicted over several months, the property was vandalized. It was in such terrible condition that it took three months for the lender to bring it up to salable standards. Then the lender had to pay an agent a commission to sell it.

Lenders look at you as a walking bag of risk factors. The rate you pay, the costs you are charged, and the kind of loan you get are all calculated to keep the preceding scenario from happening.

Why Lenders Covet the Single-Family House

The least risky piece of real estate for lenders to loan on is the single-family detached home, one that is occupied by the owner and used as his or her principal residence. Lenders love a free-standing structure, stick built, sitting on its own lot in a pride-of-ownership neighborhood. The more it conforms to the other houses in the neighborhood, the better.

This is why I am fond of buying older three-bedroom, two-bath houses in established pride-of-ownership neighborhoods. If lenders like them so much, who am I to argue?

Single-Family Residences (SFRs) Are the Most Marketable Pieces of Real Estate Today

1. A person living in an SFR is in the highest-demand, most marketable piece of real estate today, the holy grail. It is easiest to sell if the lender has to take it back.
2. By far, single-family detached houses have the largest number and variety of loan programs available today.
3. SFRs are usually in stable neighborhoods.
4. Houses tend to hold their value well in down markets.

The loan pricing for these properties is more favorable. Condominiums, planned urban developments (PUDs), duplexes, triplexes, and fourplexes (two to four units) can be good to live in and invest in, but lenders consider them more risky. Here is why:

- Condos and PUDs can:

  1. Have homeowners' associations that can go broke raising monthly assessments, causing increased financial strain in the borrower.
  2. Have increases in association dues because they don't keep a cap on expenses.
  3. Mismanage the project's overall maintenance.
  4. Lose value more rapidly in down markets. Prices fluctuate more.
  5. Resemble apartments more closely, particularly mid-rise and high-rise projects.
  6. Be older buildings in continual disrepair.
  7. Be surrounded by other high-density projects, reducing livability.
  8. Be built poorly.
  9. Be subject to construction-defect lawsuits.
  10. Have homeowners' associations that are very unfriendly to renters. I have seen such associations harass residents simply because they did not own their property.

- Two- to four-unit buildings can:

1. Not be located in desirable areas.
2. Have their value derived solely from the income they produce. If rents go down, so goes their worth.
3. Not be located in residential neighborhoods.
4. Be older.
5. Have no owner occupants.
6. Tend to get beat up more by tenants.
7. Be mismanaged by amateur landlords who do not know what they are doing.
8. Have higher maintenance costs.
9. Be harder to finance.
10. Be resold only to another investor who may be smarter than you.
11. Be very crowded. Dense living is not conducive to people staying a long time, so tenants tend to be more transitory.

2

WHY LENDERS LOVE PAPER, OR HOW MANY TREES HAVE TO DIE FOR MY LOAN?

Lenders live on paper. You may be a great person—good looking with beautiful kids and a loving spouse—but unless you can prove it on paper, forget it.

INCOME
You Say You Make a Good Living? Prove It

If you are a salaried employee, you will need to provide the name and address of your employer(s) for the last two years. The gross income you have received has to be documented with the last two years' tax returns,

W-2 forms, and one month's worth of pay stubs. If you got a raise, lenders will work with what you currently make.

If you are self-employed or receive commissioned income, lenders will need to see all the pages of your last two federal income tax returns to find your net income, not your gross. Borrowers in business for themselves who write off many of their expenses may save a great deal on taxes but will show less income to qualify. You may need to provide copies of your 1099 forms, and depending on the source of your income, you may need to provide K-1 forms. Your Schedule C will be scrutinized because depreciation and single, one-time capital expenditures may be added back in. This can boost your income. Lenders may ask for a profit and loss (P&L) statement.

If you receive pension income or Social Security income, you will be asked to provide a statement of benefits and a letter of award.

If you receive alimony or child support, you will need to provide a copy of the divorce decree.

If you receive rental income, lenders will ask for the current leases or the last two years of Schedule E from your 1040 forms.

DEBTS
But I Don't Owe That Much

Most people do not know exactly what they owe, but it's all there on the credit reports obtained from the three credit-reporting agencies—TransUnion, Experian, and Equifax. Your mortgages, lines of credit balances, amounts due on your credit cards, how much you owe on your car, and any personal loans all show up on the credit reports. You would be surprised to learn how many people don't want to know how much they owe.

The payments on your loans are also on the credit reports. Lenders will use those payments to add up your total outgo. Then they figure your total debt-to-income ratio (more on how to figure your ratio later) to see if you fall within their guidelines.

1. If something on a report shows as unpaid and you paid it, you need to prove it with a letter from the creditor admitting that the creditor reported it in error.
2. A car loan with less than 10 months left will not be counted.
3. If an account appears and it is not yours, it can be taken off. The credit company your lender uses will call up the creditor and verify that it is not your Social Security Number attached to the account.
4. If you had a bankruptcy and accounts were mistakenly left out of the bankruptcy, they can be removed. You will need a copy of your discharge of bankruptcy.

You cannot hide what you owe. It's all right there on your credit report, so you might as well add it all up right now and get a handle on your debt. You may not be happy looking at the debris of your past, but if you are in denial about your debt, you need to face it.

Rapid Rescoring

It is very common to see credit reports with mistakes and omissions. Your credit score can be raised immediately if the reporting error is verified by the credit company. As a mortgage broker, I can get you a more favorable loan because I will take your supportive documentation to my credit company and get your score corrected within hours. But you will need to report the error to the credit bureaus to have it removed from your credit records permanently.

Rapid rescoring is wonderful because when a creditor admits a reporting error or a mistaken entry, rapid rescoring will raise your credit score dramatically and in the process save you untold thousands of dollars.

I had occasion to use rapid rescoring when a bank had mistakenly reported that I was over 30 days late on a house payment. Just one late mortgage payment is so deadly that my credit score plunged more than 90 points! Incensed at this error, I called the bank and immediately had them fax me a deletion letter saying that it was the bank's fault. My credit company had my report rescored two hours later.

EVEN MORE PAPERWORK

The paper chase starts at loan application. Besides the records you supply, loan files end up stuffed with appraisals, escrow/attorney instructions, inspection reports, title insurance policies, deeds, termite reports, surveys, letters of explanation, and lender directives ad infinitum. A competent loan officer should be able to tell you in advance just about everything you need to come up with.

It is a lot less aggravating to dig through your records just once rather than piecemeal. Here are most of the other items that lenders will want from you:

- A copy of your signed purchase contract
- The listing agreement
- A copy of the earnest-money check
- A copy of your hazard insurance declaration page
- Letters of explanation as required

A LOT LESS PAPERWORK REQUIRED IF YOU GO STATED INCOME, STATED ASSET, OR NO DOC

Less paperwork is required in this situation because you do not have to document your income and/or assets. Stated income, stated asset, and no documentation (no doc) loans are more expensive because lenders assume more risk if they cannot verify your income or assets. They are used mostly for the self-employed wage earners who simply do not have enough income to qualify.

You may command privacy or do not want to go through the hassle of dredging up income documentation. No tax returns or bank statements are required if you do not want to release potentially sensitive information.

I will cover exactly what these loans are and how they work in more depth later.

HOW LENDERS LOOK AT YOU
He Who Has the Money Sets the Rules

It is all about risk. With all the sophisticated risk models, data-gathering sources, and other research they conduct, lenders can tell with a high degree of certainty the chances of you going into foreclosure or serious delinquency. In Chapter 3 you will see firsthand how we price these risk factors in the loan itself. To help you understand these risk factors and to see how the loan process relates to you, think of it in terms of four C's.

The Four C's

1. *Collateral*. The property itself.
2. *Capacity*. How well you can pay back the mortgage with respect to your income and other debts.
3. *Credit*. Your record on how you have repaid other creditors.
4. *Cash*. How much you are putting down and how much you have in reserve.

Collateral

Real estate loans are secured by the collateral. The property is the collateral. The worth of it, the kind of structure it is, and the surrounding neighborhood make a big difference in the pricing of your loan and in whether you can get financing at all.

1. *Value.* What will the property appraise for? The more money the lender puts in the deal, the less you do, and therefore the more risk the lender assumes. This is called *loan-to-value* (LTV) *ratio*. There is a big difference in pricing if you put 5 percent down (95 percent LTV ratio) versus 20 percent down (80 percent LTV ratio). With refinances, if you cash out all your equity (100 percent LTV ratio), you pay a lot higher interest rate. The more of your money or equity you put in the deal, the more the lender likes it.

2. *Appraisal.* Your property's appraisal sets the value of the collateral. The lender does not know your property from another. The lender trusts the licensed appraiser's opinion of value but will review the appraisal when it comes in. Sometimes lenders will *cut* the value. This is especially common in depreciating markets or wildly inflating ones. Or a lender may not like a particular appraiser because he or she has inflated property values in the past. It is not unusual to see such renegade appraisers be blackballed.

3. *Cash out.* You pay a slightly higher rate if the lender is loaning you cash out of your refinance as opposed to lowering your existing interest rate and getting no cash out. You present a higher risk if you are cashing out your equity.

4. *Owner-occupied.* Do you live in it? Non-owner-occupied investment property is much more risky for a lender and goes into foreclosure more often. This is why:

- In times of financial hardship, lenders know that you will let go of an investment property before you walk away from the house you live in. This is a proven fact.
- Most people do not know how to manage tenants, so their rental cash flow is endangered.
- Rental properties get beat up more by the tenants, which can affect long-term value and marketability of the collateral should the lender have to take it back at foreclosure.
- Many lenders will not lend on a vacant house because it could be vandalized, and it is harder to insure.

5. *Condominiums.* This is one of the most common risk factors, as I discussed previously. Here is why:
   - Many condo homeowner's associations do not manage their cash reserves well, resulting in higher assessments. They overspend.
   - Many condos are nonwarrantable condos. If a project is less than 50 to 60 percent owner-occupied, many lenders will not even lend on them. Those that do can have some very high rates. Foreclosure rates are much higher in condo complexes with a large number of absentee owners. Mostly tenant-occupied buildings are not kept up as well as owner-occupied projects.

6. *Multiunits.* Duplexes, triplexes, and fourplexes go into foreclosure more often than houses, so the interest rates can be much higher, and bigger down payments may be required.
   - The value of two- to four-unit buildings is derived from the income they produce. If the rents go down, so goes the value.
   - In flat or depreciating markets, units tend to lose their value quicker.
   - Units are harder to sell because there are fewer buyers who want them. People buy houses to live in them; investors buy units to make money. Which segment has more buyers?

- Vacancies matter. If one or more units is vacant, you may not get a loan.

7. *Second homes.* Although you may use the property as a vacation home or weekend getaway, you are not living there. Lenders consider second homes as an extension of your primary residence and therefore less risky.
   - Second-home pricing is slightly higher than that for owner-occupied properties but a lot better than pricing for non-owner-occupied investment property.
   - A word here for those of you using second-home loans for investment property. You cannot count rental income to qualify, and you will have to sign an addendum when you sign your loan documents guaranteeing that the property is not going to be a rental and that you and only you will occupy the property.

8. *Leased land.* Most residential property is legally attached to the lot it sits on. This is called *fee simple.* But some buildings sit atop land the building owner does not own. The lot belongs to another owner who leases it out. Somebody else owns the dirt underneath. This can definitely detract from the value of the property, and the loan will cost you more. This is called *leasehold.*
   - Lenders will want to see a copy of the land lease and will not loan for longer than the lease will run.
   - When the lease expires, will the owner of the lease renew, and, if so, at what price? Owners usually do, but this adds enough uncertainty to make the loan more expensive.

9. *Manufactured/modular homes.* This is such a gray area. In the past, you had to get a high-interest personal loan to buy a manufactured home. A manufactured home is not built on the lot site but assembled in pieces at a separate location. It is then trucked to the site. In the past, the quality of construction was greatly suspect, but it has improved recently, so more

lenders are doing them. As long as the home is fixed on a foundation and can get Fannie Mae certification, you probably can get a residential loan on it, but it will cost you more.

10. *Seasoning issues.* Many lenders have dictated that you must own the property for at least 6 to 12 months before you can refinance. During this time, they will use the original purchase price, not the current market value. A lot of people try to refinance their newly purchased property. In a highly appreciating market, lenders can become suspicious of people who want to pull cash out quickly. A rapid run-up in housing values makes lenders nervous. The seasoning requirement has been relaxed by many lenders in recent times, however.

11. *Volatile markets.* If the property is in a market undergoing rapid change, you may pay more for a loan because the market is volatile. Some lenders may suspect the housing growth in a certain area to be unsustainable.

12. *Soft markets.* If the lender identifies your market to be stagnant or soft, or if there are a lot of foreclosures in the area, the lender may elect to cut all LTV ratios by 5 percent or more. He or she will lend 5 percent less money in order to have more security for the loan.

13. *Zoning.* Your property must be zoned appropriately for a lender to loan on it. If it is in a single-family-home neighborhood, the zoning designation is R-1, duplexes are R-2, and so on. You cannot have fourplexes in R-1 neighborhoods.

   • Some people add more units than the city allows; these are called *granny flats* or *bootleg units.* They add illegal, nonconforming units to gain more income. Lenders see any prohibited addition as a possible safety hazard whose electrical wiring and plumbing systems may not have been built to code.

14. *Permits.* Any property additions have to be inspected and approved by the city. The appraiser will have to go to the city

building department and pull permits. Unprofessional work-manship can present safety hazards.

15. *Major renovations.* Some minor repairs are okay, but lenders do not want to see bare drywall, cement floors, or exposed electri-cal wires. Don't tear your house apart and then apply for a loan.

16. *Room configuration.* Odd layouts that do not conform to other properties in the area will not be accepted. Unusual floor plans can make the collateral less marketable if the lender gets the property back after a foreclosure.

17. *Square footage.* If the property is not compatible with sur-rounding housing in terms of square footage, this affects future marketability, and you will pay more.

18. *Rural property.* Houses on large acreages with not many other houses around them are hard to sell. Interest rates can be higher on these properties.

19. *Listing history.* If the property has been listed for six months and has not sold, many lenders will be reluctant to lend on it.
    - On a cash-out refinance, lenders fear that an owner who cannot sell the place may want to cash out all his or her equity and walk.

20. *Chain of title.* Lenders are wary of people buying properties and quickly reselling them at highly inflated prices.
    - If you are buying from a seller who has been the owner of record only for a few months, watch out if your price is sub-stantially higher than what he or she paid for the property. If you do not get renovation receipts from the seller to jus-tify the increased value, you may not get a loan.
    - Lenders also watch out for people who fraudulently resell a property at inflated prices to straw buyers with suspicious appraisal information. Straw buyers are fictitious buyers who take part in phantom real estate transactions in order to profit by defrauding the lender.

Lenders want to lend money to people who keep their loans a long time. If a loan is paid off rapidly, lenders don't make as much money. For this reason, *flippers* (people who quickly buy, fix, and resell property for profit) will use private financing or get a *hard-money loan* (a high-interest-rate loan based solely on the property's equity and not on the borrower's income and credit). I have used these high-cost hard-money loans on occasion for short-term purposes but later put on long-term financing with much better terms.

Capacity to Repay the Loan

Here is where we talk about debt-to-income ratios. Your monthly income goes to service your monthly debts. Lenders want to see no more than 28 to 36 percent of your income dedicated to your monthly mortgage payment, property taxes, hazard insurance, private mortgage insurance (PMI), homeowner's assessments (HOAs), and principal, interest, taxes, and insurance (PITI).

They also want no more than 36 to 45 percent of your income going to your house payment *plus* the rest of your debts. The monthly payments on your credit cards, cars, student loans, alimony/child support obligations, negative cash flows from rental properties (remember, lenders only count 75 percent of rental income because of a 25 percent vacancy and maintenance factor), and any other debts are computed here.

Example 1: Let's say that you and your wife make $10,000 a month, your house payment is $3,000 a month, you pay $200 a month on your credit cards, and you have two car payments that total $800 monthly. Thus $10,000 income divided by $3,000 PITI is 30 percent. A little less than a third of your monthly gross income goes to your house payment. Lenders like that. However, $10,000 income divided by $3,000 PITI plus $1,000 other debt is 40 percent. Now you are paying 40 percent of your income for your house, cars, and credit cards. The debt-to-income ratio is 30/40. So far, so good. But wait, there is more.

Example 2: Now you want to buy three rental properties with a breakeven cash flow. The rent is $1,000 a month, but the lender counts only $750 dollars. Lenders discount your rental income by 25 percent because of a vacancy and maintenance factor. Each property now has a $250 monthly negative cash flow. Thus $10,000 monthly income divided by $3,000 PITI is 30 percent. However, $10,000 monthly income divided by $3,000 PITI plus $1,000 other debt (credit cards, car payments) plus $750 negative cash flow is 47.5 percent. Now the debt-to-income ratio is 30/47.5. This is not good because the last number is too high. *You cannot qualify for a fully documented loan because the lender is saying that you are now overloaded with debt.*

You think that you are doing a good thing by buying a few rental properties. You are building long-term wealth, but why is the lender discounting your cash flow by 25 percent? Lenders figure that you do not get to keep all your cash flow, and they are right. The actual negative cash flow can be much more if you have property in a soft rental market that does not rent quickly or if you have inferior professional property management.

The 25 percent vacancy and maintenance factor can be a lot less for seasoned investors who know how to manage properties and screen tenants.

Banks Are Tough on New Investors

Amateur landlords typically have more vacancies and overspend their maintenance budgets more than experienced property holders do. Banks know this and may toughen requirements for new investors who may not know what they are doing. If this is you, you may want to pay close attention when I talk about managing tenants in Part 2. Banks like seasoned pros, and I will teach you how to be one in Part 2 because I have learned from the best.

When that 25 percent vacancy and maintenance factor comes into play, it does not take too many rental properties to push your ratio too high. When this happens, you end up having to go with *stated income loans.* More about stated income loans later.

Let's go back to your income. For fully documented loans, lenders count some income sources and not others.

Lenders Will Count

- Salary verified by W-2 forms and paycheck stubs. If you have changed jobs within the last two years, they want no large gaps in employment.
- Less than two years' income if the borrower is starting work in a new profession where he or she just completed education.
- Overtime and bonuses if they are expected to continue.
- Self-employed income verified by the last two years of tax returns with Schedule C. Some write-offs, such as equipment depreciation and single, one-time capital expenditures, can be added back in to income. A year-to-date profit and loss statement may be required.
- Social Security and/or disability income if it is expected to continue for two years. You need to have a letter of award from the governmental entity.
- Pension and other retirement benefits verified by letter of award and/or direct deposit in your bank account.
- Interest and dividend income documented by two years of 1040 forms with Schedule B.
- Tax-free income such as Social Security can be grossed up to 110 to 125 percent.
- Alimony and child support expected to continue for two to five years depending on the type of loan. This is verified by divorce decree and canceled checks.
- Rental income subject to the 25 percent discount as discussed earlier.
- IRA income. Early withdrawals are subject to 10 percent penalty, however.

Lenders Will Not Count

- Any cash compensation.
- Roommate rent.
- Part-time income if not received for two years.
- Proceeds from the sale of stock or other property unless that is the borrower's profession.

There are many other sources of exotic income. To use any income source, it all boils down to a very simple rule: It must be *reliable, recurring, verifiable, and extend into the future for at least two to five years.*

And do not change jobs in the middle of your loan application.

Credit

Lenders care very much how you have handled your credit in the past. They figure that how you have treated other creditors is how you will treat them. You would not believe the calls I get from people trying to explain away their bad credit. It is never their fault.

Banks don't care if your divorce cratered your credit or if you lost your job or took ill and got behind on your car payments and credit cards. It doesn't matter to them if your kid quit making payments on a loan that you cosigned. You are going to pay more for your loan.

In the old days, we could possibly sway an underwriter to approve a loan by using a well-crafted letter explaining why somebody didn't pay his or her bills. No longer does an underwriter listen to hard-luck stories because now there are *credit scores* or *FICO scores*. And this is a good thing because credit scores have proven to be surprisingly accurate in predicting how people will pay their bills in the future.

The three credit-reporting bureaus—Experian, TransUnion, and Equifax—rely on the credit-scoring model developed by the Fair Isaac Company (FICO). Using a scale of 350 to 850, the FICO credit-scoring system gives lenders a pretty accurate idea of the chances of your defaulting on a loan.

The higher your FICO score, the better loan you get. There is great information available on the Web site www.fairisaac.com that shows the impact of FICO scores on the cost of your loan.

However, there are many exceptions. For instance, I can get very good pricing for people with lower scores if there are other compensating factors. I provide a list of compensating factors at the end of this chapter.

FICO scores are calculated from a lot of different credit data in your credit report. These data can be grouped into the following five categories:

- *Payment history* (35 percent)
    1. Account payment information on specific types of accounts (credit cards, retail accounts, installment loans, finance company accounts, mortgage, etc.)
    2. Presence of adverse public records (bankruptcy, judgments, suits, liens, wage attachments, etc.), collection items, and/or delinquency (past-due items) and severity of delinquency (how long past due)
    3. Amount past due on delinquent accounts or collection items
    4. Time since (recency of) past-due items (delinquency), adverse public records (if any), or collection items (if any)
    5. Number of past-due items on file
    6. Number of accounts paid as agreed
- *Amounts owed* (30 percent)
    1. Amount owing on accounts
    2. Amount owing on specific types of accounts
    3. Lack of a specific type of balance in some cases
    4. Number of accounts with balances
    5. Proportion of credit lines used (proportion of balances to total credit limits on certain types of revolving accounts)

6. Proportion of installment loan amounts still owing (proportion of balance to original loan amount on certain types of installment loans)

- *Length of credit history* (15 percent)
  1. Time since accounts were opened
  2. Time since accounts were opened by specific type of account
  3. Time since account activity
- *New credit* (10 percent)
  1. Number of recently opened accounts and proportion of accounts that are recently opened by type of account
  2. Number of recent credit inquiries
  3. Reestablishment of positive credit history following past payment problems
- *Types of credit used* (10 percent)
  1. Number of (presence, prevalence, and recent information on) various types of accounts (credit cards, retail accounts, installment loans, mortgage, consumer finance accounts, etc.)

Do You Have a Credit Score?

Of the hundreds of credit reports I see per year, here are the *most common reasons* people have low FICO scores. These are ranked in order of occurrence.

1. *Recent credit-card lates,* mostly through carelessness
2. *Collection accounts,* where a bill dispute is never resolved, and the account holder gets stubborn and refuses to pay
3. *Too high a balance* on credit cards
4. *Age of credit accounts* too young; not enough long-term credit
5. *Closing credit accounts* in the mistaken belief that this will improve credit scores
6. *Tax liens*

7. *Bankruptcies* where not all accounts were included that were supposed to have been cleared off the credit report

When you apply for a loan, lenders will run all three credit reports. Of the three scores, they will take the middle score and use that one to qualify you. If there are two or more borrowers applying for the loan, they will count the lowest middle FICO score.

You should make sure that the information in your credit report is correct. Not only is your credit score based on this information, but lenders also review this information in making credit decisions. Review your credit report from each credit reporting agency at least once a year and especially before making a large purchase, such as a house or a car. To request a copy, contact the credit-reporting agencies directly:

- Equifax: (800) 685-1111, www.equifax.com
- Experian (formerly TRW): (888) 397-3742, www.experian.com
- TransUnion: (800) 888-4213, www.transunion.com

You should treat your credit report like gold and guard it closely. Your credit history (i.e., mortgages, lines of credit, credit cards, car loans, and student loans) stays on your report for 7 years, and matters of public record (e.g., bankruptcies, tax liens, foreclosures, and judgments) last for 10 years. Lenders see this as an example of your financial character.

Bankruptcies and Foreclosures

Most loan programs require that bankruptcies and foreclosures be two to three years old to qualify you for the good rates. I see far too many people take the easy way out and declare bankruptcy. Then, when they want to buy a house, they whine. If you have a bankruptcy, make sure that you are very proactive in establishing at least three new accounts as soon as the bankruptcy is discharged. To get the good rates, lenders typically want to see three new lines of credit established for at least three years.

Do Not Let Your Sordid Past Stop You from Becoming Wealthy

If you have bad credit and want to invest in real estate, do not fear. Fifteen years ago, it happened to me. My first real estate venture did not end well. I had the idea of buying a three-unit building, living in one unit, and renting out the other two so that my tenants would help to make my house payment. Have you ever had this idea?

It was good to try it, but I failed in my execution of it. I did not know much about real estate investing or managing tenants. The building was in a not-so-good neighborhood, and I found it hard to attract good, stable, and long-term tenants. I always seemed to have a unit vacant. The quality of tenants I had was low, and they ran me ragged. After one and a half years of money flying out the door, I gave the property back to the bank. Besides now having a foreclosure on my credit report, I had several tax liens as well. I thought I was done with real estate.

My first real estate venture rated a grade of F—as in *foreclosure.*

It took several years of diligent rehabbing of my credit to qualify to buy another property. I opened up several new credit cards and made a deal with the tax collectors that if I paid the liens off, they would delete them from my credit report. Three years later, I bought my residence and have since bought many more houses.

If this resonates with you, do not despair. You can repair any bad credit history. All it takes is time and a change in behavior.

Cash and Other Liquid Assets

Money in the Bank? Where Did You Get It?

The more cash you've got, the better you look. The old saying that the more you look like you do not need to borrow money, the easier it is to get it is true.

You will need to provide all pages of all checking, savings, and passbook accounts for the last two months. For brokerage accounts, the most recent quarterly statement will suffice.

- *Seasoned funds.* Lenders want to see that it is *your money* being used for the down payment and closing costs. They want to make sure that somebody did not quietly slip you the money. The source of any recent large deposits will have to be accounted for if you are using the money for the down payment. If your down payment is coming from a previous sale, the lender will need a copy of your closing statement. Lenders will use the two-month average balance that shows in your accounts. It is okay if your down payment money is coming from a refinance loan or a line of credit. Refinancing existing property and using the cash out to buy more income-producing property is wonderful use of your equity and a great wealth-building tool. You will need to tell your lender about it so that he or she can include the increased payments in your debt-to-income calculations.
- *Cash reserves in your accounts.* Anywhere from two to six months of your future house payment may be required after your transaction has closed.
- *Seller contributions.* Seller contributions to down payments up to 6 percent can be accepted. If the seller wants to kick in up to 6 percent of the purchase price to go toward closing costs, that's fine, but the lender still will want to see the buyer have at least 5 percent of his or her own funds involved.
- *Gift funds.* For many people buying their first primary residence, a blood relative may give them the down payment. Lenders are okay with this so long as a letter is signed indicating that it is not a loan. The donor's source of gift funds will have to be documented via bank statements and canceled checks.

Basically, lenders care that you have the ability to save and that you don't blow everything you make. Your proven ability to save is a very strong compensating factor.

Compensating Factors

Almost all loans have some flexibility. I have gotten clients qualified for very good loans with debt-to-income ratios as high as 55 percent, FICO scores as low as 580, and no money in the bank!

Here is a short list of compensating factors that lenders will consider:

1. No debt or little debt
2. Excellent long-term credit
3. Large amount of liquid assets left after closing
4. Proven ability to save
5. Long-term job stability
6. Good potential for an increase in income
7. Work done toward an advanced degree
8. Large down payment, low LTV ratio loans
9. Small increase in housing expense; low payment shock

Here is where the skill and experience of your mortgage person comes into play. He or she should know very well what loan underwriters will accept and what they won't. Often I can get my underwriters to waive many conditions and make the process go more smoothly because I give them a lot of business.

HOW LENDERS PRICE LOANS
Why Your Neighbor Gets One Rate and You Get Another

I spend a lot of my time pricing loans, so I can give people accurate rate quotes. I get rate sheets every day from wholesalers telling me what the prices of their loans are that day. When people call me to ask what rates are, there is no simple answer. Everybody's loan profile is different according to collateral, credit, capacity, and cash. I have to ask people a lot of questions before I can give them an accurate quote.

Many loan officers don't know how to read a rate sheet. This is sad but true for my profession. Have you ever ended up with a rate that was higher than what you were quoted originally? Part of the reason for this lies with the inexperience or incompetence of the loan officer.

The other part of the answer is greed. The higher rate you get when the loan closes, the more profit the loan officer makes. *There are some tricksters in my business who will deliberately mislead you, so I actually worry about people when they go somewhere else.*

To help you to avoid mistakes, let's go through an actual wholesale rate sheet. We will have to spend some time on how loans get priced according to different risk factors.

Looking at the Rate Sheets

I have to tell you that most of you probably won't get this on the first try. Reading the rate sheets that I get every day and factoring in all the rate adjustments, or *hits,* can be very complex and tedious. Wholesale lenders have gotten so tired of retail loan representatives making mistakes and misquoting rates to their customers that they have developed computerized software, or "pricing engines," to make it easy. One error can result in a big difference in the rate you get and the money you pay.

Follow me closely over the next several paragraphs and you will understand exactly how loans are priced. The following rate sheet is very simplified because it shows how lenders will charge for the risk factors that they think are important.

In column 1 of the rate sheet, you can see where the interest rate is. Look for the number 5.375. That is the interest rate for a 30-year fixed-rate loan posted that day. The rates are graduated in the form of fractions—one-eighth percents. Decimally, those one-eighth percents are expressed as 0.125. One-eighth of a percent is 0.125, two-eighths is 0.250, three-eighths is 0.375, four-eighths is one-half or 0.500, five-eighths is 0.625, and so on.

Rate Sheet

Base Prices Only (Add-Ons Not Included) / Adjustments

Rate	16 Days	20 Days	40 Days	65 Days	Description	Amount
7.625					3-4 units	1.000
7.500					95% 2-unit purchase	0.500
7.375	-3.875	-3.750	-3.500	-3.375	Cash-out 70.01–80%	0.500
7.250	-3.875	-3.750	-3.500	-3.375	Cash-out 80.01–90%	0.750
7.125	-3.875	-3.750	-3.500	-3.375	CLTV>90%	0.250
7.000	-3.875	-3.750	-3.500	-3.375	Credit score<620%	0.500
6.875	-3.875	-3.750	-3.500	-3.375	Manufactured homes	0.500
6.750	-3.875	-3.750	-3.500	-3.375	N/O/O 75.01–80%	2.000
6.625	-3.875	-3.750	-3.500	-3.375	N/O/O 80.01–90%	2.500
6.500	-3.875	-3.750	-3.500	-3.375	N/O/O up to 75%	1.500
6.375	-3.750	-3.625	-3.375	-3.250	Loan amounts<$100,000	0.500
6.250	-3.250	-3.125	-2.875	-2.750	Loan amounts<$50,000	1.500
6.125	-3.000	-2.875	-2.625	-2.500		
6.000	-2.750	-2.625	-2.375	-2.250	Comments: mimimum loan amount $30,000	
5.875	-2.250	-2.125	-1.875	-1.750		
5.750	-1.500	-1.375	-1.125	-1.000		
5.625	-1.125	-1.000	-0.750	-0.625		
5.500	-0.500	-0.375	-0.125	-0.000		
5.375	0.125	0.250	0.500	0.625		
5.250	0.750	0.875	1.125	1.250		
(1)	(2)	(2B)				(3)

Next to those rates in column 2 is the cost to get that rate. *Points* buy the rate (1 point is 1 percent of the loan amount). For the rate of 5.375 percent in column 1, there is a number (–0.125) right next to it in column 2. This tells us that to get a rate of 5.375 percent, it will cost us one-eighth of a point, or 0.125 percent.

Look at the number 5.250 percent right below 5.375 percent. If you want to get a rate of 5.250 percent, it will cost you three-quarters of a point, or 0.750 percent. If you borrowed $400,000 at 5.25 percent, it would cost you $2,800 more. Pretty costly, huh? Wouldn't you want 5.375 percent? It only costs 0.125 percent, or $500. Of course you would want it because it makes the most financial sense. Even though you would get lower payments at 5.250 percent, it would take a very long time for that $31 lower payment to make up the additional cost of $2,800—74 months or 6.18 years of payments to be exact. That $2,800 would better spent toward buying a house or another higher-yielding investment.

Now let's throw a wrinkle into our example. See the adjustments on the far right. Those are the risk factors, and these price adjustments also are expressed in points. All these hits make your loan more expensive because they represent more risk to the lender. Let's say that $400,000 is from an 80 percent LTV ratio cash-out refinance. Your real estate is worth $500,000, so you are borrowing 80 percent of its value, or $400,000. Borrowing that $400,000 on a three- or four-unit property will cost you more—1 point more. Because your property is a three- to four-unit building and not a house, the loan automatically costs you $4,000 more (1⅛ points, or 1⅛ percent). Four-unit buildings tend to go into foreclosure more often than houses for the reasons I mentioned in Chapter 1.

Now let's say that your four-unit building is one you do not live in. You do not occupy it, and you are holding it for investment. It is now non-owner-occupied (NOO). Loan companies know that if you do not live in it and have some financial hardship in your life, that rental property will go into foreclosure before the house in which you live does.

Thus, for the pleasure of owning this four-unit non-owner-occupied building, the lender is charging you 1 point for the units and 2 points because you will not be living in it. You could pay this total of 3 points, or $12,000, out of pocket to get that 5.375 percent rate. Most people don't.

Maybe you don't want to pay that $12,000 at all. You could pay a little higher rate. Say, instead of paying 3.125 percent (3⅛ percent), you could pay 0 points if you take a higher rate of 6.125 percent. Move up the rate sheet in column 2, and next to the 6.125 percent rate there is the number –3.000. This negative number is called a *rebate*, and you can use it to pay the points you do not want to pay out of pocket. Most people do not want to pay a lot of points because they have better things to do with their money.

So that is how lenders price out loans. I know that all the numbers may be dizzying for some people. Just know that the more you borrow, the higher your LTV ratio, and the lower your credit score, the more it's going to cost you. If you have a condo or a multiunit property, there will be more points, or you may accept a higher rate and use the rebates to pay for the adjustments. If you don't show your tax returns or bank statements, the less the lenders know about you, and the more risk they assume.

The Longer You Reserve Your Rate, the More It Costs

You can lock in your interest rate for a longer period of time. Until now, all our pricing has been good only for 15 days, which means that this loan has to fund in 15 days. You would need to have everything done—all loan conditions signed off, title report in, appraisal and inspection contingencies met, walkthrough, and so on. A lot needs to be done on your real estate transaction, so you need a longer lock to get the rate you want.

If you want the 5.375 percent rate to be good for 30 days, you will have to pay 0.125 percent (⅛ percent), or $500, more. Look at column 2B for 30-day pricing, and for the 5.375 percent rate, you see the number 0.250 (¼ point), or $1,000, to guarantee that rate. This is the cost—the longer the lock of the rate, the more it's going to cost. For 55 days, the rate is guaranteed, but it will cost you an additional 500 point ($2,000) to get it (column 2C).

I will talk more about rate locks later in this book.

All the Different Risk Factors

So now you can see how lenders charge for riskier loans. There are more adjustments on the rate sheet, such as cash out, 80.01 to 90 percent (0.750), credit score under 620 (0.500), for manufactured homes (0.500), and so on. Lenders adjust for the risk factors in the points you pay, in a higher interest rate, or in a combination of both. There are a whole host of other risk factors that lenders will tag you for—stated income, lower credit scores, higher loan amounts, mid- and high-rise condos, condo hotels, states with soft/volatile markets, and higher debt-to-income ratios are just some of the hits you can be charged when it comes time to price your loan.

Interest rates that appear on the rate sheets I get from my wholesalers change every day, sometimes more often if the market is very volatile. Some of my vendors have specialized loan programs with hyperspecific underwriting guidelines, so the rate sheets can get very involved. This is why many consumers get rate misquotes from inexperienced or inept loan hacks. I say only use loan people who have been highly recommended to you.

GOOD NEWS FOR BORROWERS: THE MORTGAGE MARKET HAS BECOME SAFER FOR BIG BUSINESSES BECAUSE THEY NOW ASSESS RISK ACCURATELY

The American consumer benefits hugely from having a vast array of loan products available to meet every need and customizable for his or her individual situation. In Chapter 3 we will see why there has been such a sudden growth of loans. While sophisticated risk models were unavailable to the investment bankers of yesterday, today large companies, insurance companies, pension funds, and foreign central banks can invest in these securitized mortgage bundles because they can know quickly how their investments are performing. How many loans are going into default, if the payments are late, and how soon those loans are refinanced are just some of the feedback they get. The 30-day late payment a borrower misses in Indiana can show up on a computer screen in China.

It's all about the yield mortgage bankers get. One of the reasons investment bankers can choose the kind of loan portfolio they want to invest in is that now they can price the risk factors. They may favor NOOC stated income loans with high credit scores for a time, or primary residence loans with lower credit score may come into favor. They will offer attractive pricing to get the kinds of loans they want or make the products they do not want more expensive. Making money on seemingly risky loans is now possible because their risk models accurately assess risk better than ever before.

3

THE HOME LOAN EXPLOSION

ALL THE DIFFERENT KINDS OF LOANS

I have never seen so many different kinds of loan programs as I do today. It is amazing. Just for me to keep up with them is a full-time job. I can only imagine the confusion of the regular person out there who buys two or three residences in his or her life or the investor who may buy more property but still is overwhelmed.

The loan business is no different than any other industry. Companies strive continuously to expand their market. Mortgage companies that safely capture a larger market share will prosper as long as they do not go too far out on a limb. This home loan explosion has been very beneficial because more people get to own homes, and home ownership is a pillar of this nation's wealth.

There are five reasons for this growth:

1. *There is extreme competition in the secondary marketplace to generate more loans.* In America, we have the most sophisticated financial market the world has ever seen. After any loan funds on a mortgage banker's credit line, the vast majority of them are sold in large bundles on the secondary market. These loans are securitized in $5 million to $100 million lots that are bought and sold as fixed-income products called *collateralized loan obligations* (CMOs). If you have invested in Ginnie Mae or Freddie Mac mutual funds, you have money invested in home loans. These investors continually assess the risk of how many of these loans are likely to become delinquent. Investment bankers such as Fannie Mae and Freddie Mac will aggressively create new loan products to meet new niches so that they can stay in business. People having more choice in terms of types of loans tend to buy more property and refinance more often.

2. *Fixed income investors have insatiable appetites.* There is a great deal of domestic and international capital pouring into mortgage products. Home loans secured by American real estate are perceived to be almost as safe as U.S. Treasury bonds. U.S. Treasury bonds, despite what you hear, are widely known as the safest fixed-income investment in the world. Thus overseas banks invest heavily in these CMOs because the yield is 2 to 3 percent higher than that of Treasuries. There has to be enough fixed-income product to meet the wave of capital coming to our shores. New loan products are invented to satisfy this demand.

3. *The easy-to-reach market is already saturated.* Loans are becoming ever more specialized to target different segments of customers. People wanting the most popular 30-year fixed-rate loan already have been reached. Since that market is limited, investors continually ask themselves, What do homeowners and

investors need? What products will the marketplace bear with acceptable risk?

- *Alternative-A credit loans ride to the rescue.* Stated income loans; no documentation (no doc) loans; 100 percent interest-only financing for 2, 3, 5, and 7 years; 30-year fixed-rate super-jumbo loans above $1 million; and 5 percent down and 0 percent down investor loans for two to four units are just some of the loan products that have appeared. Most of the loans I have done in recent years are of this variety.

4. *There are more customers.* With American home ownership approaching an all-time high of 70 percent, more people need to be accommodated:

- *More baby boomers.* According to the U.S Census Bureau, the 76 million strong baby-boomer generation provided a significant boost to home ownership levels in recent years. As this demographic ages, its members will transition into their prime home ownership years, pulling home ownership rates higher.

- *High immigration.* Strong levels of immigration have contributed to rising home ownership. Studies show that recently arrived immigrants tend to buy homes more quickly than people already here. And their native-born children comprise the fastest-growing population segment, so they too will be in the market to buy houses.

- *Governmental accommodation.* Lower-income consumers are likely to become homeowners because of recently passed affordable-housing legislation.

- *Echo boomers.* The echo-boomer generation, born between 1976 and 1994, numbers 72 million. This generation is just now starting to rent apartments and buy cars, and many will soon be home buyers, as studies show this wealth-savvy generation tends to purchase homes earlier.

- *New households forming.* Economists at Harvard University's Joint Center for Housing Studies believe that these immigrants and echo boomers will form between 13.4 million and 14.5 million new households, and most of them will buy real estate.

   This trend has fueled over $2 trillion in annual new loan originations in recent years—*$2 trillion!* Definitely more loan products will have to be created to cope with this demographic surge.

5. *Housing is becoming more expensive.* The median house price in the United States is $208,240, and this is expected to rise 5 percent to $218,700 in 2006, according to David Lereah, chief economist of the National Association of Realtors. In highly appreciating markets such as California, the median house as of December 2005 hit $479,000, a 13.0 percent increase. New loan products with higher loan amounts will become increasingly common.

A CAVEAT HERE

The main dark spot on the horizon is the 100 percent loan-to-value ratio interest-only loans. In the future, more and more borrowers will have to rely on housing appreciation instead of on the "forced appreciation" that paying down their loans provides. Similar to when car makers came up with the concept of leasing cars instead of owning them, loan companies have created ways for people of average incomes to afford nice houses. The main problem with interest-only loans is that the loan never pays off. More people will have to "rent" a loan just as they lease a car. In the next section I will discuss the pros and cons of interest-only loans, as well as all the other loan types.

   Before we delve into the features of all these different loan programs, I want you to keep the following scenario in mind.

INTRODUCING JOHN Q. BORROWER

I am going to be using an imaginary borrower so that you can see how different loan scenarios play out. John Q. Borrower is buying a house for $400,000 and is putting 20 percent down, so his loan amount is $320,000. It is a single-family residence that he will live in. He is getting a 30-year fixed-rate loan at 6 percent and is paying 1 point. Property taxes for his new house will be approximately $417 per month, and his hazard insurance should be around $40.

As we go along, I will tell you what his payments are so as to help you see the pros and cons of each kind of loan. I also will add variations so that you can see how they work. In addition, I have to tell you that not every loan is available for every situation, and I will try to note this as we progress.

FIXED-RATE LOANS

1. *30-year fixed (30/30).* This a 30-year loan that is amortized over 30 years. Some loans don't pay off in 30 years, such as a 30-year loan that comes due in 15 years (30/15). More on this later.

   The 30-year fixed-rate loan is by far the most popular type of loan during times of low to moderate interest rates. This is for good reason: People like certainty of payment. They want to know what their payment will be. A lot of people don't like surprises, so when rates dip, there is a rush to refinance to lock in low fixed rates.

   John Q. Borrower's principal and interest (PI) payment at 6 percent is $1,918. With his taxes and insurance (TI) added in, his PITI is $2,375.

2. *20-year fixed (20/20).* Less popular than the 15-year fixed-rate loan, this loan is chosen by people who want to pay off their loans more quickly but who cannot afford the payments for a 15-year loan. If the 30-year rate is 6 percent, the 20-year rate would be around 5.75 percent.

    John Q. Borrower's PI payment at 5.75 percent is $2,246, and his PITI is $2,703.

3. *15-year fixed (15/15).* This is the second most popular fully amortized fixed-rate loan. A lot of people want to get their houses paid off as soon as possible, so they choose this option, which is especially popular in times of very low rates. If the 30-year rate is 6 percent, then the 15-year rate would be about 5.5 percent.

    John Q. Borrower's PI payment at 5.5 percent is $2,614, and his PITI is $3,071.

4. *10-year fixed (10/10).* This is not a very popular loan because it really jacks up your payments. I have done very few 10-year fixed-rate loans. If the 30-year rate is 6 percent, the 10-year fixed would be around 5 percent.

    John Q. Borrower's PI payment at 5.0 percent is $3,394, and his PITI is $3,811.

Personally, I am not a big fan of the 20-, 15-, or 10-year fixed-rate loans. Some people are determined to get that house paid off as quickly as possible. That's fine. If my clients want such loans, I will get them, but far too often their personal circumstances change, and they cannot afford the higher payments. Then they come back to me wanting to refinance out of those loans. I think it makes more sense to get a 30-year loan and pretend that it is a 15-year loan.

Pretend that it is a 15-year loan? That's right. You can figure out what your payment would be if you wanted to pay off your loan in 15 years. John Q. Borrower's payment on his 30-year loan would be

$2,700 a month if he wanted to pay it off in 15 years. *This is only $86 a month more than the 15/15 fixed-rate loan quoted above.* You don't pay that much more in interest by taking a 30-year fixed-rate payment, and the flexibility it gives you is worth it. If you lose your job or get sick, you can easily lapse back to the lower 30-year fixed-rate payment.

I like to always think about the yield that my money is making for me. If the interest rate on your 15-year loan is 5.5 percent, the yield by paying that house off more quickly is also 5.5 percent. I can think of lots of places where I can get a better return than 5.5 percent—buying more houses, for example.

Here are the pros and cons for fixed-rate mortgages:

Pros

1. Payments are predictable and certain.
2. They are good for long-term holds—if you are going to stay in your house for at least seven years.
3. A fixed payment will look cheaper years from now if rates are up.
4. You will have inflation and the time value of money working for you.
5. Every payment goes to principal and interest.
6. It is good to lock in rates while they are low.

Cons

1. You are locked into a higher payment, particularly with the 10-, 15-, and 20-year fixed-rate loans.
2. They are not worth it if you are going to refinance within seven years.
3. If you think you are going to sell soon, don't take a long-term fixed-rate loan.
4. They are bad if rates are high or going down.

ADJUSTABLE-RATE LOANS

Adjustable-rate loans, or variable-rate loans, require more discussion because there are more things to watch out for. They have more moving parts, and you need to understand how they work.

Before I address the different kinds of adjustable-rate loans, I need to talk about indexes, margins, interest-rate caps, conversion options, start rates, and negative amortization.

Indexes

Your loan payment will change according to the underlying financial index. As the index goes up and down, so goes your payment. You need to be careful because some indexes are more volatile than others. You can compare the behavior of these indexes by looking at some of the financial Web sites in Appendix 1.

These rates are all published in the *Wall Street Journal.* The most common indexes are:

1. *6-Month London Interbank Offered Rate (LIBOR).* This is based on rates that contributor banks in London offer each other for interbank deposits. From a bank's perspective, deposits are simply funds that are loaned to them. *This is a very quickly moving index.*

2. *1-Year Treasury (T-Bill) rate.* This index is an average yield on U.S. Treasury securities adjusted to a constant maturity of one year, as made available by the Federal Reserve Board. *This is slightly less volatile than the LIBOR.*

3. *11th District Cost of Funds Index (COFI).* This is the weighted average of the cost of borrowing (funds) to member banking institutions of the Federal Home Loan Bank of San Francisco (the 11th district). The index rate tends to lag market interest-

rate adjustments and is relatively stable. *The COFI is the least volatile index and the most preferred.*

4. *Prime rate.* This is the interest rate banks charge their most creditworthy customers (usually the most prominent and stable business customers). The rate is almost always the same among major banks and moves in tandem with the Federal Reserve when it moves its rates. This index is used most often for home equity lines of credit (HELOCs). I will talk about HELOCs later.

Let's take a look at where the *Wall Street Journal* showed these indexes to be as of August 13, 2004:

1. 6-Month LIBOR: 1.98 percent
2. 1-Year T-bill: 2.10 percent
3. 11th District COFI: 1.75 percent
4. Prime rate: 4.50 percent

To illustrate how quickly each index moves, let's take a look at their values as of February 8, 2006, just 1.5 years later:

• 6-Month LIBOR: 4.89 percent
• 1-Year T-bill: 4.66 percent
• 11th District COFI: 3.29 percent
• Prime rate: 7.50 percent

Let's see. In approximately 1.5 years:

• The 6-month LIBOR moved up 2.91 percent.
• The 1-year T-bill rate moved up 2.56 percent.
• The 11th District COFI moved up 1.19 percent.
• The prime rate moved up 3.0 percent.

Did you notice how the Treasury index and the LIBOR index moved up twice as fast as the 11th District COFI? And did you see how the prime rate index moved up almost three times as fast?

Which index would you prefer your house payment to be based on?

Margins

The margin gets added to your index to determine your interest rate. That is, index + margin = your interest rate. This is very important to banks because the margin is where banks make their profit. Usually the margin that gets added to your rate runs from 2.25 to 3.5 percent. It can vary widely depending on the index used and how risky a borrower you are.

Let's say that good ole John Q. Borrower is an A borrower with good credit and a stable income, so his margin is only 2.75 percent. When we add his index and margin to get the fully indexed rate, we find that his principal and interest payments on his loan of $320,000 are as follows:

1. For the 6-month LIBOR at 7.64 percent, his PI payments are $2,268 and his PITI payments are $2,685.
2. For the 1-year Treasury rate at 7.41 percent, his PI payments are $2,217 and his PITI payments are $2,634.
3. For the 11th District COFI rate at 6.04 percent, his PI payments are $1,926 and his PITI payments are $2,643.
4. The prime rate generally is not used for first mortgages.

You will notice that the PI payment for an adjustable-rate loan ranges from $1,926 to $2,268 per month, considerably more than the 30-year fixed-rate payment of $1,918 per month. Most of the time, the payments on adjustable-rate loans are considerably less. Usually, John Q. Borrower could expect these variable-rate loans to save him about $200 to $300 dollars a month. But no more, not now, because not all loans are built the same.

Let's finish our discussion of how adjustable-rate loans work before I tell you why not all loans are built the same. Using adjustable-rate loans always has depended on your risk tolerance, the type of index, and your overall strategy.

Caps

Caps limit how much your interest rate and payment can go up or down. What happens if rates go through the roof? Will your payments go up so fast that you will lose your house? Probably not, because there are limitations on what the rate can do each time the loan adjusts and how high it can go for the lifetime of the loan.

1. *Lifetime caps.* Over the lifetime of a loan, rate increases are limited. Usually, the cap is 6 percent over the start rate. If John Q. Borrower's loan has a start rate of 6.04 percent with his payment being at $1,926, at 12.04 percent, his payment will never exceed $3,301 a month.

    Watch your lifetime caps if you intend to keep this adjustable-rate loan long term. *I am really not too concerned with rates ever reaching the lifetime cap.* If rates are going up and I have a variable-rate loan, I know that that is a risk I take. If rates are rising, so usually are rents and income that offset my loan risk.

    There are some very attractive loan programs where the lifetime cap never exceeds 8.95 percent. Not everybody can qualify for them, however.

    Also, be aware that caps on HELOCs usually are around 18 percent, the same as credit cards. More about HELOCs in Chapter 7.

2. *Adjustment and payment caps.* Whether your loan adjusts once a month or once a year, it is usually limited to 2 percent per year. If your rate now is 6.04 percent and interest rates are going through the roof, the highest your rate would be next year would be 8.04 percent. For example, John Q. Borrower's loan payment of $1,935 at 6.08 percent would increase to $2,365 at 8.08 percent.

    Some loans have payment caps; that is, the payment itself cannot increase more than 7.5 percent a year. This type of cap is most common with negative-amortization loans. If John Q. Borrower's payment is $1,935, this type of payment cap holds the payment to $2,080. If rates are going up, the payment itself cannot increase more than 7.5 percent per year.

NEGATIVE-AMORTIZATION LOANS AND LOW START RATES (TEASER RATES)

Ever hear on the radio or read in the newspaper, "If you are paying more than 1.95 percent on your loan, you are paying too much! We can lower your payment and save you thousands of dollars on your loan!" Yes, you can save thousands of dollars on your loan, *but there is no free lunch.* These artificially low payments come at a price. What you do not pay in interest gets added on to the loan principal. Your principal balance is not being paid down but actually is growing. This loan is going through negative amortization (expanding loan balance), not positive amortization (principal being paid down with every payment).

John Q. Borrower is delighted to pay only $1,174 a month to buy his $400,000 property at the 1.95 percent interest rate. Wow, what a great deal! But he does not see that while the actual fully indexed market rate for his loan is 6.08 percent, the interest on that loan comes in at $1,621 a month. He does not realize that $447 a month is added on to his loan balance. His principal is *going up* $5,368 that year, and possibly more if interest rates are on the upswing.

PICK-A-PAYMENT OR OPTION ADJUSTABLE-RATE MORTGAGES (ARMS)

These kinds of loans have been around a long time. When John Q. Borrower makes his payment each month, the coupon the lender sends him usually has three payment options:

1. *Deferred interest payment.* The payment is $1,174. This is the lowest option with negative amortization.
2. *Interest only.* The payment is $1,621. Only the interest is paid.
3. *Full principal and interest.* The payment is $1,935. Part of the payment goes to principal, and part goes to interest.

Are negative amortization loans bad? Not necessarily, because they give you options. Now I will list the pros and cons.

Pros

1. You can qualify for more house.
2. They are fairly safe if the index is good.
3. They are good if you are comfortable with interest-rate risk.
4. You have flexibility of payment—you can go deferred interest or not.
5. They are good for short-term holds—if you are going to sell soon.
6. They are good if you are going to refinance soon.
7. They are best when rates are high and declining.
8. Some can be assumed.
9. They are safer in appreciating markets.

Cons

1. There is uncertainty of payment from month to month or year to year.
2. They are bad when rates have no place to go but up.
3. They can pile deferred interest onto principal.
4. They can be very costly because you can end up paying interest on the accumulated deferred interest. Paying interest on interest is expensive.
5. They have high lifetime interest cap.
6. There can be sudden payment shock if interest rates rise rapidly.

7. There is the possibility of negative equity, especially in declining markets.

8. Most have prepayment penalties.

HYBRID LOANS

A hybrid loan is a combination of a fixed-rate loan and an adjustable-rate loan. The loan is fixed for an initial period of time, and then it becomes adjustable. Such loans usually come in four varieties. To get an idea of how low these fixed payments can be, I have included the payments.

Remember that John Q. Borrower's 30-year fixed-rate loan is at 6 percent, and his payment is $1,918 monthly. Or he could get:

1. *3/27 (5.75 percent).* Fixed for 3 years and then variable ($1,867) for the remaining 27 years

2. *5/25 (5.875 percent).* Fixed for 5 years and then variable ($1,892) for the remaining 25 years

3. *7/27 (6.25 percent).* Fixed for 7 years and then variable ($1,970) for the remaining 23 years

These rates are not exact, and I use them only to illustrate the spread between the programs. If you choose this kind of loan, watch for what sort of variable-rate loan it changes into at the end of the fixed-rate period. Be careful of your index and margins.

Pros

1. You can qualify for more loan at the lower payment.

2. You have the best of both worlds—lower payments and a fixed rate.

3. They can be designed with a lower fixed payment if you need a fixed payment for a short period of time.

4. They are good in a rising-rate environment.
5. Some of the principal is paid off with every payment.

Cons

1. There is uncertainty of payment after the fixed period is over.
2. There can be a higher payment than with the adjustable.
3. You don't know if your adjustable will be the best kind to get.
4. Your plans can change, and then you may be in for higher rates and payments when it turns into an adjustable.
5. They are bad if rates are declining, but better than a 30-year fixed-rate loan.
6. You probably will have to refinance.
7. You may have to sell the property if payment shock is too much.

INTEREST-ONLY LOANS

All the preceding hybrid loans can come with the interest-only feature. Your payment only pays simple interest, and the principal balance remains the same. You can pay additional sums on the principal whenever you wish (subject to the prepayment penalty if you have one; more about that later).

John Q. Borrower wants to pay interest only. If a 30-year fixed rate is 6 percent, then shorter-term fixed rates likely will be:

1. *3/27 (5.75 percent)*. Fixed for 3 years and then variable ($1,533)
2. *5/25 (5.875 percent)*. Fixed for 5 years and then variable ($1,566)
3. *7/27-(6.25 percent)*. Fixed for 7 years and then variable ($1,666)

Thirty-year fixed-rate loans also come with an interest-only feature. The interest-only feature usually lasts for 10 to 15 years, and then payments are principal and interest for the remaining 20 years.

30/30 (6.0 percent). Fixed for 30 years. The loan does not go to adjustable. The rate remains fixed for the entire 30 years ($1,600 interest only)

What Happens to My Interest-Only Loan When It Becomes Adjustable?

With many lenders, the interest-only loans have one nasty drawback that deserves further mentioning. At the end of the initial fixed term, they become an adjustable-rate loan and adjust to market rates. Two years ago, if you took a 3/27 loan with interest-only at 4.125 percent (which is where they were 2 years ago), next year you would start paying principal and interest for the remaining 27 years. There is usually a 2 to 3 percent cap on how much the rate can go up. You do not know where interest rates will be next year.

Some lenders will allow you to keep paying interest only, not the full principal and interest payment. The loan never pays off. You have to examine the loan documents closely to know for sure.

Example: John Q. Borrower took an interest-only 3/27 loan 2 years ago at 4.125 percent, and his interest-only payments are $1,100 monthly. Now it is next year, and the rate is 6.125 percent. John Q. Borrower's fully indexed rate (index plus margin) is also 6.125 percent, and he has 27 years left on his now-adjustable-rate loan. His fully indexed principal payments now are $2,021 for the remaining 27 years. If rates go up, so will his payment. Thus John Q. Borrower's payments increased $921—*an 84 percent increase per month.*

Will this happen to you?

Interest-Only Loans Are a Possible Powder Keg

Quite a jump in payments, is it not? If there is equity in the property, the vast majority of borrowers will refinance out of this loan, according to industry insiders. Or they will not be able to absorb the jump in payments and will have to sell the house. *If there is not enough equity in the house, then they are stuck because they cannot refinance or sell. In coming years, many of these loans will go into default.* Make sure that you read all your loan documents to know what you are getting.

Will I Pay More Interest Overall with an Interest-Only Loan?

Unfortunately, the answer is yes. On a fully amortizing loan, part of every payment goes to principal, and part goes to interest. With interest-only loans, your payment is all interest. It is simple interest, not fully amortizing interest. Simple interest is calculated differently.

For example, John Q. Borrower takes a three-year fixed-rate interest-only loan at 4.125 percent. He is glad to see that he is only paying $1,100 a month interest only instead of $1,550 a month that pays full principal and interest payments. He figures that he saves $450 a month, which over three years works out to be a savings of $16,200. This is not a bad deal if he invests that money.

But he pays more interest overall. Over three years, he has paid $39,600 total interest ($1,100 × 36 months). If this were a self-amortizing loan, where part of every payment goes to principal and interest, the total interest he would have paid is $38,584. This is a difference of $1,015 over three years, or about $28 a month.

And his principal would have gone down $17,247 during those three years.

I know that these numbers can make your eyes cloud over. Just know that there is more than meets the eye with these interest-only loans.

Pros

1. You can qualify for more loan at the lower payment.
2. You can buy more house.

3. You can make a property cash flow better.
4. Your house payment is more affordable.
5. You have the best of both worlds—a low interest-only loan, and the payment is fixed for a period of time.
6. You can design a lower fixed-rate interest-only payment if you need a fixed rate for a short period of time. This is especially useful if you do not know how long you are going to keep the property or if you are going to refinance at a later date to pull cash out.
7. You can pay on loan principal when you want.
8. Good in a rising-rate environment or when rates are high.

Cons

1. There is uncertainty of payment after the fixed period is over.
2. There can be a higher payment than the adjustable.
3. There are high lifetime caps.
4. You don't know if the adjustable will be the best kind to get.
5. Your plans can change, and then you get stuck just when you want to get out of the loan. You may be in for higher rates and payments.
6. They are bad if rates are declining because you will be locked into a higher fixed rate.
7. Big payment shock is possible when the interest-only period is over.
8. You probably will have to refinance or sell the house if you can't make the payments.
9. You may not be able to refinance if there is not enough equity.
10. There is no forced savings—no money is paid to the principal if you do not have the discipline to make voluntary principal payments.
11. You pay more interest than you would on a fully amortizing loan.

NOT ALL INTEREST RATES ARE CREATED EQUAL ON THE LOANS YOU GET

It is complex to explain exactly why the rates on a 30-year fixed-rate loan can be much higher or lower than the rates on an adjustable-rate loan and the 2-, 3-, or 5-year hybrid loans. And sometimes, depending on the behavior of the Treasury bond market, the rates may not be much different at all.

You need to know this because it will make a difference in what kind of loan is best for you.

As we have seen, interest rates change all the time. But 30-year fixed rates change on a much different schedule than those of hybrid and adjustable-rate loans. This is so because the most common adjustable-rate indexes, namely, the LIBOR, the 11th District COFI, the Treasury bond rate, and the prime rate, are roughly reliant on what the shorter-term Treasury bond market is doing. Hybrid and adjustable loan rates are determined by what the two-year Treasury bond market is doing that day and whether the Federal Reserve is tightening or loosening the credit markets. As these yields go up and down, so goes your house payment.

Most of the time, there is a significant gap between the interest rates in adjustable-rate loans, shorter-term fixed-rate loans, and longer-term fixed-rate loans. But not all the time. We have just seen that adjustable-rate and hybrid loans can be no bargain in today's market. Recently, the interest rate on an adjustable rate was only 0.25 percent less than that of a 30-year fixed-rate loan, which reflects the narrowing yield spread between short- and long-term Treasury markets. As recently as early 2005, the spread was wider at 2 to 3 percent.

Now the spread is only 0.25 to 0.75 percent. This is a rare thing, but it is happening. Short-term money is almost as expensive as long-term money.

THE ALLURE OF ADJUSTABLE RATES IS DISAPPEARING

Thus the advantage of adjustable-rate and hybrid mortgages is fading. The spread could decline even more in coming years as foreign investors continue to invest in 10-year Treasury bonds, keeping 30-year fixed-rate mortgages near historic lows. This offers some consolation to anyone who has been waiting to buy because the rise in long-term rates has been much slower than that in the short-term rates.

Let's hammer this point home even more. When short-term yields on the 2-year Treasury are going up noticeably and the long-term yields on the 10-year Treasury are not, you can have a flat or even an inverted yield curve. Short-term money is almost as expensive as long-term money. When this happens, there is little difference in the interest rates you pay for your adjustable-rate/hybrid loans and for a 30-year fixed-rate loan.

If you can lock in your interest rate for 30 years at almost the same price as for a shorter time of 5 years, would it not make sense to get a longer term fixed-rate loan? In this way, you take interest-rate risk off the table because long-term interest rates are such a bargain. The less you pay for your debt over time, the more wealth is added to your net worth.

BEST TIMES TO
USE EACH LOAN

Responsible use of debt is a very important part of wealth building. Knowing the right kind of loan to get will lower your holding costs of the property you buy significantly. Personal situations and goals are different for everybody, so the kind of loan you want will differ from that of your neighbor.

Here are some things to think about when you are choosing the best loan for you:

1. What are your long-term goals for the property?
   - Will you be moving soon?
   - Do you need to know with certainty what your payment will be?
   - How is your tolerance for risk? Is it high or low?
   - Are you going to refinance and pull cash out in the coming years, or are you going to leave the loan alone and pay it off?

- Do you need quick cash flow for your investment property?
- Are you going to sell it? When?
- How much do you have in cash reserves?
- Is your employment stable?
- Are you going to live there?

2. What is happening in the economy should make a major difference in the type of loan you get. What is the present economic climate?
   - Do you think interest rates are going to go up or down?
   - Are present-day interest rates high or low?
   - Will the area where you invest continue to be economically progressive?

Best Times to Get an Adjustable-Rate Loan

1. When you want to get the lowest payment possible
2. When you have to qualify for the most house possible
3. When you have a high tolerance for risk
4. When you need immediate cash flow
5. When you think rents or personal income will rise to cover a future higher payment
6. When you are okay with the concept of possible negative amortization
7. When you may be moving out of the property soon
8. When you are going to sell or do a 1031 tax-deferred exchange within two to three years
9. When you are going to quickly fix and sell property
10. When you will be refinancing soon
11. When you think interest rates may be going lower
12. When present-day interest rates are high
13. When you have the ability to pay principal off in chunks in coming years (large cash reserves)
14. When you are not sure about the area and possibly will sell in the future

Best Times to Get an Intermediate-Term Fixed-Rate (Hybrid) Loan

1. When you want lower payments but also want less short-term volatility
2. When you have medium risk tolerance—gambling that interest rates could be lower at the end of the fixed-rate period when it switches to adjustable
3. When you don't need to have the absolute lowest payment and still will have acceptable cash flow
4. When you need to know what your payment is for the next five to seven years
5. When you are definitely going to sell or do a 1031 tax-deferred exchange in the next five to seven years
6. When a cash-out refinance is in your future and you have a good use for the cash
7. When you are not sure where interest rates are going
8. When you are going to hold on to the property for the five to seven years
9. When interest rates might be lower in five to seven years, when the loan changes to adjustable, or when you refinance
10. When you don't need to have the loan paid off quickly to get the property free and clear
11. When the area may be good, but you don't know if you want to have a property in that area forever
12. When you think rents will increase

Best Time for Interest-Only Loans

1. When all the above are true
2. When you need to get the payment as low as possible because the interest-only payments are considerably less than the fully amortized principal and interest payments
3. When you need the best cash flow possible

4. When you are okay with the probability of higher payments in the future

5. When you don't care about reducing your loan balance

Best Time for Long-Term Fixed-Rate Loans

1. When you are going to keep the property forever

2. When you are not likely to sell or do a 1031 tax-deferred exchange

3. When you need to be certain of what your payments are

4. When you are not likely to refinance within 10 years

5. When you can afford higher payments

6. When you want to pay off the loan to make the property free and clear (possibly want 10/10, 15/15, or 20/20 year fixed-rate loan to pay the loan off in 10, 15, or 20 years)

7. When you have low risk tolerance

8. When present-day interest rates are low

9. When you are expecting future interest rates to be higher

10. When you are familiar with the time value of money

11. When property rents are likely to increase

12. When you want to use higher principal payments as a forced savings account

13. When you have good cash reserves

14. When you have high personal income

STATED INCOME LOANS, STATED ASSET LOANS, E.Z. DOC, AND NO DOC LOANS

If you do not qualify using your income, do not despair. No money in your bank accounts? No problem. No job? You can get a loan. For a price, lenders have available many different types of loans to help you get a house or refinance an existing loan.

When you can fully document your income and assets with tax returns and bank statements, you will get the best rates. But when you cannot show enough income to qualify, you must start approaching the stated income loans to qualify.

When I first started doing loans, there were only fully documented loans and E.Z. doc loans, and they were not all that easy to get. The loan companies who did the E.Z. doc loans had mostly adjustable-rate loans, and those loans were few in number. The rates were not that great, and the underwriting requirements were strict. Nowadays, these loans are commonplace and not that much more expensive—sometimes only ¼ to ½ percent higher than the fully documented rate. You can get very attractive fixed rates.

For these no income qualifying loans, it is important to distinguish three categories:

1. Stated income loans
2. Stated asset loans
3. No doc or E.Z. doc loans

Stated Income Loans

If you are self-employed and do not show enough income on your tax returns, this is the loan for you. Or if you are a wage earner and your income is too low to qualify, this is also the best loan for you. If you have bought many income properties, you eventually will fall into this category.

To qualify for this loan, you merely *state* the income high enough to qualify. You just plug in enough income into your debt-to-income ratio calculation to get you to qualify. You might ask how it is that loan companies will even look at your income if it is fictitious. It is not your real income.

Loan companies suspect this, so they verify everything else. It is a more risky loan for them, so you pay a higher rate. You need better credit, more cash for your down payment, more cash reserves, and more equity in your house. This phantom income figure also must pass the reasonability test. If your verified occupation is being a janitor and you have to state your income to be $10,000 a month to qualify, that may not fly past the underwriter. In these cases, the loan underwriter has wide discretion.

Notice that I said your *verified* occupation. For stated income loans, the loan companies will verify the fact that you have been self-employed for at least two years. This can be documented via a business license or letter from your CPA.

If you are salaried, you will need to be employed continuously at the same company or the same occupation for two years with no significant gaps in your employment. The quality control department at the loan company will telephone to verify your employment status.

E.Z. Doc and No Doc Loans

What if you do not even have a job? No problem, because then you can get a no doc loan. Don't need a job; don't need any money in the bank. *You leave that section on your loan application totally blank.* It can be done, but you will pay a higher rate, and the underwriting requirements become even more stringent.

Loan underwriters will want to see higher credit scores, more equity, and more cash for the down payment and for reserves. No doc loans are not available for all situations.

Stated Asset Loans

No money in the bank? You say that you do not have two months of seasoned funds in the bank verified by bank statements? No problem, because then you simply *state* enough assets on your loan application.

You may not have enough money in the bank to buy a house, so you are going to quietly borrow it from a friend or a relative. This is a very common occurrence. If the down payment money has not been sitting in your bank account to be seasoned for at least two to three months, banks will assume that you borrowed it and start asking more questions.

Payment Shock May Be an Issue

Lenders want to make sure that you are not getting in over your head, so if they cannot verify your cash assets, they will want to know how much your past house payment or previous rent was. If your new house payment is way higher, you may not get the loan. Most lenders want your new house payment to be no more than 200 percent higher than what you had before, or payment shock will become an issue.

As you can see, stated income, stated asset, and no doc loans have become increasingly commonplace. Loan companies have become more aggressive because of the home loan explosion and because more people do not fit the standard borrower profile. These new loan programs represent significant strides in the area of alternate-A loan programs.

$$\boxed{5}$$

BUYING HOMES AND INVESTMENT PROPERTIES: WHAT TYPE OF LOAN SHOULD YOU GET?

M any people are mystified by the loan process. They talk to loan agents, get confused and bogged down with loan jargon, and get quoted different rates and costs with different down payment requirements. How do we make sense of this mess? The answer always revolves around your individual goals and what you intend to do with the property.

Here are some tips:

1. *Know the time value of money.* If interest rates are low and you can possibly afford it, lock in long-term rates. If you are not intending to refinance or sell within 5 to 7 years, get a 30-year fixed-rate loan. The payment that will be fixed for a long time

will not look so big 5 to 10 years from now. Inflation erodes the value of money over time. The house payment you get today that seems so impossibly high will look a lot less 5 to 10 years from now because tomorrow's dollars are a lot cheaper than today's dollars: $1 today will only buy 86 cents worth of goods in 5 years, assuming today's inflation rate of 3.2 percent.

The future inflation rate could be much greater given the increasing costs of food, energy, and health services. This makes knowing the time value of money all the more important.

2. *The less of your own money in the deal, the better—to a point.* The more of the bank's money in your house, the more leverage you have working for you. Thus 100 percent financing gives you the most leverage, but you pay the highest rates because the lender is assuming all the risk. For example, the rates for 5 percent down, stated income investment property loans can be 2 to 4 percent higher than if you put 10 percent down. Weigh out all the extra interest you will pay.

3. *Can you comfortably afford the payments?* Will your income increase in coming years, making the house payment more affordable? Did you buy your investment property in an area where rents are increasing so that you can better afford the payment later?

4. *How much can the payments go up later?* A five-year fixed-rate interest-only loan gives you lower payments now, but how much can they go up? Will interest rates be higher or lower in the future?

5. *How much of a down payment—0, 5, 10, or 20 percent or more?* Is your main goal to lower the payments to be comfortable? Or do you want to put less down and hang on to more of your cash for emergencies or to buy more property? It is a balance between getting those payments as low as possible and keeping as much cash in your pocket as possible.

6. *Will you refinance or sell soon?* If you are going to refinance or sell the property within 5 to 7 years, you do not want a 30-year fixed-rate loan. You do not need to pay the higher interest rate that a 30-year loan brings. By taking a straight adjustable-rate loan or a short-term hybrid loan, you can customize the loan to be fixed for any time period you want. If you really want to lower your payment and you don't care if your loan pays off, all these options can be done interest-only.

7. *Are you going to serial refinance?* Many people refinance every year using their houses as an ATM machine (bad). Or they will use their cash-out proceeds for business investments, to buy more houses, or to make property improvements (good). Just know that if you continually refinance, you start the clock over each time you do. And you will have more loan costs in your future.

A Delicate Balancing Act

There are no easy answers to what is the best loan for you. You have to decide what your comfort level is because it is always a delicate balancing act between:

1. *Debt.* How much are you willing to take on? Can you make the payments?

2. *Cash.* Do you have enough of a buffer for unforeseen emergencies?

3. *Income.* Will you have enough personal income/cash flow to make the payments? How certain are you that your earnings will rise or your rents will increase?

4. *Equity.* Will your equity expand to enhance your net worth or for a future refinance?

5. *Risk of future economic events.* Where will interest rates be in the future? Is the city where you invest or live economically progressive?

THE SHRINKING DOWN PAYMENT
100 Percent Financing Loans: Should You Get Them?

You don't need much money these days to buy a house or even an investment property. There are 100 percent financing loans available if you want to buy a house, a condo, or a four-unit building. It can be your primary residence, or it can be a rental property. You can go full doc or stated income.

Lack of savings for a down payment is the number one barrier of entry for people wanting to own real estate. From an investment standpoint, the less money of your own you put down, the higher the return on your investment. There are a lot of advantages to putting very little of your own money down.

Rates are higher for these loans, though. The less of your own funds you put into the deal, the more risk for the lender, and the higher rate you pay. How much higher? That depends. Depending on the type of loan, your rate can be anywhere from 1 to 6 percent higher than a 10 percent down loan.

You will need to have money for closing costs and two to five months' payments left over after escrow closes.

Let's take a closer look. Most 100 percent financing programs are in the form of two loans: an 80 percent first and a 20 percent second (otherwise known as an *80/20 loan* or a *piggyback loan*). Most people buying their first house are short of funds. The types of loans they take are of the two-, three-, or five-year fixed-rate loans for the first mortgage. At the end of the fixed-rate term, we have seen how high the payments can go. There is a danger that such borrowers may lose their houses because of the increased payment.

Investors like the low to no down payment loans because there is less money out of pocket. They will take the two- and five-year fixed-rate loans because of the increased cash flow. Because of the payment "pop" at the end of the fixed term, they will have to refinance or go with the adjustable-rate loan. Hopefully, there is enough equity to bail them out.

The terms on the second mortgage can be an equity line of credit, a 15/15 fixed, or a 30/15 fixed. When I say 30/15, I mean that it is a 30-year loan amortized and paid off like a 30-year loan, but it comes due in 15 years. The second mortgage balloons in 15 years and becomes payable. It is usually the most popular choice because the rates are lower.

The rates on the second mortgage can be significantly higher. I have seen rates on seconds for a 100 percent stated income investment property loan go as high as 13 to 15 percent and 10 to 11 percent for a primary residence purchase.

Remember John Q. Borrower? He was putting 20 percent down on his $400,000 purchase, making his 30-year fixed-rate payment $1,816 at 6 percent interest. Let's say that John had very little money, stated income, and wanted 100 percent financing.

A likely scenario for his $400,000 purchase would be as follows:

- For an 80 percent first of $320,000 (30-year fixed) at 6.25 percent, the payment is $1,970.
- For a 20 percent second of $80,000 (30 due in 15) at 10 percent, the payment is $702.
- His total payment is $2,672 a month, $754 higher than if he had 20 percent down.

This is for a stated income loan, so the above rates would have been a little lower for a full documentation loan.

CONCLUSION

Just because you can get a no or low down payment loan does not mean you should get one. Everybody's situation is different, but I will make some general recommendations regarding these types of loans:

1. Be sure that you can afford the payments, especially if the loan changes to adjustable.
2. If you have the money, compare what your payments would be if you put more down.
3. If you have a much better use for the money, consider putting less down. Make sure you will be comfortable with the higher loan payments.
4. Don't forget that you will need to have money for closing costs and reserves.
5. Be okay with the possibility of negative equity if property prices do not rise.
6. You may not be able to refinance out of your existing loan, so be satisfied with the terms you have.
7. Be aware that these types of loans are good options for high wage earners with little savings.
8. If taking out one of these loans is the only way to get into real estate, do it.

6

SHOULD I REFINANCE MY PROPERTY?

Your home is your castle, but it can also be your bank. Four of five homeowners refinanced their homes and pulled cash out in the United States last year, according to Freddie Mac.

Most people have four goals to accomplish when they refinance their existing loans:

1. Lower their interest rate and payments
2. Take cash out to invest in income-producing assets or a business
3. Improve their home
4. Pay off bills and convert nondeductible consumer debt to tax-deductible mortgage debt

I rank these goals in order of benefit and importance. The best thing is to always have the lowest rate possible to reduce your financing costs. It is very good to carefully exploit the dead equity sitting in a property to buy income-producing assets. Invest in things that are going to increase your net worth. Improving the value of the real estate you now own is wise. Although paying off higher-interest-rate credit cards is good, it is not smart to charge them up again. Many people want to pay off their loans quickly, so they refinance from a 30-year loan to a 15-year loan. You can save a lot of interest if you pay off your loan quickly.

INTEREST RATES

When I became a mortgage broker in 1990, interest rates for 30-year fixed-rate conforming loans were at 10.5 percent. In three years they fell to 7.5 percent and then went up to 9.5 percent in 1995. In 1999 they fell to 6.75 percent and then rose to 8.5 percent before declining to 6.5 percent a year later. The spring of 2004 marked a low point of 4.5 percent interest rates. Pretty cheap money, huh?

In 1990, we were selling a lot of fixed-rate loans because their rates were lower than adjustable-rate loans. Rates fell so rapidly that people could save a lot of money by refinancing out of their higher variable-rate loans. Then, when rates stabilized for a time in 1996–1998, people wanting to refinance locked in lower rates before interest rates took off again, which they did in the early part of 1999. Many people, wanting to avoid the higher payments that 30-year fixed-rate loans bring, went for a 5- or 7-year fixed-rate loan at that time. You see a lot of that when markets become volatile. These short-term hybrid loans offer lower payments than a 30-year fixed-rate loan, and you know what your payment is going to be, at least for a while.

In times of stable, low interest rates, I usually advise refinancing your house with a long-term 30-year fixed-rate loan. Rates do not have to go up too much before this approach makes the most sense. When rates are rising, you can either lock in a 30-year fixed-rate loan before they go much higher or get a 5- to 7-year fixed-rate loan if you think rates are going to go a lot lower in the next 5 to 7 years.

If interest rates are high, go with an adjustable-rate loan if you think rates are on their way down. In this way, your payment will slide down with the interest rate.

If you think that you are going to need to refinance again in the next 5 to 7 years, why get a 30-year fixed-rate loan? It makes no sense because you don't need the advantage of long-term financing. The same applies if you are going to sell the house quickly. Go for an adjustable-rate loan, an interest-only loan, or a short-term fixed-rate loan if you are not going to keep that loan very long.

CASH OUT

One of the main sources for small business startup capital is the entrepreneur refinancing his or her own home. When homes appreciate in value (hopefully), this can be a ready source of cash to fuel many people's dream to own their own businesses. The ability to borrow a significant portion of your own net worth is a foundation of financial strength not found in many other places in the world.

You can use the cash to buy more investment property. I always look at the cost of the money I am borrowing and then see the yield I would receive from any property I am contemplating investing in. The total package of benefits I get from buying houses (appreciation, cash flow, tax savings, and amortization) usually far surpasses my cost of borrowing money. I tell you how to assess the yield on your investment property in Part 2.

Improving the value of the property you now own is a wonderful use of your loan proceeds. In recent years, many people have massively refinanced their real estate debt to add on to their homes or to upgrade to a better class of amenities. One of the reasons that real estate has gone up so much is that it is *worth* more. More money is in houses in the form of improvements, added amenities, and additional square footage.

Paying off high-interest consumer debt is wise, although it is far wiser not to accumulate that non-tax-deductible debt in the first place. Whatever interest rate you are being charged on your credit cards, it is usually not as good a rate as the rate on real property. The disadvantage is that if you don't pay your credit-card bill, the company charges off the debt, but if you don't make your house payment, you lose your home. You also will be paying interest on that debt for a long time.

You really don't want to use your home like an ATM machine—as many Americans do. If property values don't go up, if you lose your job, or if you get sick, you will not have the equity to fall back on, and if you are unable to make your payments, you will lose your house. It always happens in times of economic recession that bankruptcies rise and foreclosures mount.

I say pay cash for things that depreciate in value and borrow money to buy things that appreciate in value.

HOW MUCH CASH SHOULD I PULL OUT?

You could take all your cash out if you wanted to. That's right, cash-out refinance loans exist up to 100 percent loan-to-value (LTV) ratio for your home or investment property. You can do this for condos and four-unit buildings. *These 100 percent cash-out loans exist even for stated income borrowers.*

But *should* you?

I say probably not. The rates you get charged go up dramatically for 81 to 90 percent cash-out loans and even more for 100 percent cash-out loans—sometimes as much as 0.5 to 3 percent higher. Above 80 percent LTV ratio, you will pay for private mortgage insurance (more about

PMI later) or take a higher-interest-rate second mortgage. This can add hundreds of dollars to your house payments. In addition, it is always wise to keep some equity in case property values drop. There is no use in financing your real estate to the hilt!

A good, conservative strategy is to take no more than 80 percent of the value of the property, unless you have a very good use or desperate need for the cash. The more expensive financing wipes out the advantage of having the cash.

7

USING LINES OF CREDIT TO ENHANCE YOUR WEALTH AND LIFESTYLE: HOW TO AVOID THE PITFALLS

A home equity line of credit (HELOC) rightly used is a good thing to have. A HELOC is usually a second lien secured by your property. This line-of-credit loan offers many advantages but does have some serious drawbacks most bankers won't tell you about.

I use lines of credit all the time for the down payment and closing costs to buy houses. Other people will charge up their credit lines to buy furniture, cars, boats, and so on, because the interest is tax deductible. This is better than not being able to write off the interest at all. However, many of these consumers come back to me wanting to refinance out of the credit line because they have charged the line all the way up to the limit, and the balance is not going down. They have gotten used to paying only the minimum interest-only payment, which means that the loan will never pay off.

By the way, there are tax rules on how much interest you can deduct. Generally, the Internal Revenue Service (IRS) will not allow you to write off the interest on more than $100,000 in cash-out proceeds unless it is used for real estate purposes, but check with your tax advisor to be sure.

LINES OF CREDIT HAVE DIFFERENT RULES

I don't think a line of credit is a responsible use of debt if you cannot pay back what you owe. It is smarter to pay cash for things that go down in value and get loans for assets that increase in value. I only charge up my credit line if I know I can pay it back in one or two years. Line of credit debt is temporary debt in my eyes.

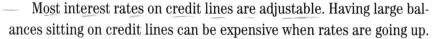 Most interest rates on credit lines are adjustable. Having large balances sitting on credit lines can be expensive when rates are going up.

HELOCs are relatively easy to get if you have equity in your house. You can get them at low to no cost, and they are easy to use. When you first get the HELOC, it can come to you pristine and unused, or the bank may fund the whole thing and give you a big check. In both instances, the credit limit is restricted by your property's loan-to-value (LTV) ratio when combined with your first mortgage. The value of the two loans together is called your *combined loan-to-value* (CLTV) *ratio.* Typically, banks will loan up to 90 percent CLTV ration on your primary residence and investment property. Sometimes the bank will go up to a 100 percent CLTV, but expect to pay a much higher margin for the privilege.

The draw period is 10 to 25 years, at which the time the bank can renew the credit line or not. Many people do not realize that the bank can opt to call the whole loan due at the end of the draw period. Can you come up with your line of credit balance in 30 days?

The prime rate is the most common adjustable index used for HELOCs. For your home, the banks usually charge zero to even a negative margin (–0.5 percent), which is good. For investment property, you will pay a 1 to 3 percent margin to compensate for the bank's added risk.

You only pay simple interest on what you borrow.

For your residence, if the prime rate is 7 percent, and you owe $100,000 and are paying 7 percent interest, your monthly payment is $583. If there is a margin of 2 percent for rental property, and the prime rate is 7 percent, your effective rate is 9 percent. Thus, if you owe $100,000 and you are paying 9 percent, your monthly payment is $750.

A line of credit loan is a lot different from a typical mortgage. A mortgage is a type of promissory note where you have agreed to pay back a fixed sum over a specific period of time in monthly installments. It is *installment debt.* The three major credit-reporting companies classify HELOCs as *revolving debt,* the same way they do credit cards.

Here is a summary of the advantages and disadvantages of using home equity lines of credit:

Pros

1. They are quick, easy, and convenient.
2. They provide easy access to cash by check or ATM card.
3. They can have a lower rate than a fixed.
4. You pay interest only on what you borrow.
5. They are low to no cost.
6. You can use debt as an asset-protection device.

Cons

1. It is easy to charge up too much.
2. Rates usually are adjustable.
3. They can have a higher rate than a fixed.
4. They have high interest-rate caps, usually around 18 percent, like credit cards.

5. Since the debt is considered revolving debt, a high balance close to your credit limit can adversely affect your credit score.

6. Your interest-only payments do not pay down principal.

7. The bank can opt to not renew a credit line, to freeze it, or to call the whole balance due if:
   - The value of the property declines to less than what is owed.
   - You are late on the HELOC more than 30 days.
   - You are late on any other credit obligation.
   - You do not pay your property taxes.
   - You move out and convert your property to a rental.
   - Your property insurance gets canceled.
   - You change jobs. A new financial statement must be submitted should this happen.

Therefore, you can see that the banks have a whole lot more power with these credit lines than with a mortgage. Will they want their money back if you don't toe the line and violate the preceding rules? Probably not if they get all their payments on time. Have they called credit lines due and payable in the past? Absolutely.

CONCLUSION

Lines of credit properly applied can enhance your lifestyle when you use them to buy things that you cannot afford now but that you will be able to afford and pay for later. Their flexibility makes them convenient. Therein lies the danger. Remember, responsible use of debt is a pillar of wealth building.

A HELOC is a great financial tool for your real estate toolbox because it can be a source of down payment funds and closing costs to buy more houses. Lines of credit, because they are revolving debt, are designed to be temporary financing devices. They should not be used as methods of permanent financing because of the disadvantages mentioned above.

8

THE THREE P'S: PIGGYBACK LOANS, PRIVATE MORTGAGE INSURANCE (PMI), AND PREPAYMENT PENALTIES

PIGGYBACK LOANS

In this situation, the borrower uses two loans, usually an 80 percent loan-to-value (LTV) ratio first mortgage and a 10 to 20 percent second mortgage to avoid the PMI premiums. The second loan "piggybacks" on the first loan, and both loans fund together. Although they fund concurrently, they are two separate loans and have two separate set of loan documents and closing costs. You will get two loan payment statements every month.

Piggyback loans for home purchases and refinances have become more popular in recent years because they avoid payment of PMI. The

PMI companies, such as GE Capital and MGIC, provide mortgage insurance that insures the lender against loss, but you pay the premiums. What a deal, huh?

PRIVATE MORTGAGE INSURANCE

Premiums that you pay for PMI can be quite steep and are not tax deductible for your primary residence. The premiums rise the less you put down because the lender has more money at risk. The more risk, the higher the PMI premium you get charged.

In recent years, PMI companies have lost as much as 40 percent of their business owing to the recent surge of piggyback loans.

How much are the premiums? PMI premiums are figured as a percentage of the loan amount. Premium percentages vary from 0.30 percent for a low-risk full doc owner-occupied high FICO score loan to a possible 1.0 percent or more for a stated income low FICO score investment property loan. Example: Loan amount of $360,000 and a PMI premium of 0.30 percent = $360,000 \times 0.30$ percent = 1,080 yearly premium; 1,080 divided by 12 months equals a 90-a-month PMI premium.

Some lenders allow you to get the PMI premium removed if the loan gets to 80 percent or less of the value of the collateral. Other lenders say that the loan has to be paid down to 78 to 80 percent of the original loan amount and that you must have had the loan for at least two years. Because of this confusion, recent congressional legislation has been enacted to require loans guaranteed by Freddie Mac or Fannie Mae to have the PMI removed when the loan gets down to 80 percent if you can prove the increased value of your house via a new appraisal or a realtor's opinion of price.

Because of the reluctance of loan companies to take off the PMI, piggyback loans have become more common. I remember back in the 1990s, when the PMI companies had more power, they used to deny a lot of loans because they got the loan back if the borrower defaulted. We could get the loans all the way to approval only to have the PMI companies turn them down. It was very frustrating.

Now it is easier to get clients approved for piggyback loans because of advances in underwriting the second loan. When underwriting the second loan, banks charge for increased risk factors, such as lower FICO scores, higher debt-to-income ratios, and non-owner-occupied properties. The second loans carry a higher interest rate than the first mortgage loans. Sometimes, in very elevated risk situations, the rate on the second loan can be much higher.

Lender-paid PMI has become popular in recent years because you can't deduct your home's mortgage insurance premiums from your tax returns. You will pay a ¼ to 1 percent higher interest rate for the privilege.

So which is better—getting PMI for your low-down-payment loan or doing a piggyback?

We will talk about three scenarios for John Q. Borrower's $400,000 purchase, where he is putting 10 percent ($40,000) down, and see where he is saving the most money. Rates and premiums quoted are not actual.

1. Piggyback—80 percent first of $320,000 at 6 percent is $1,918 a month.
2. 10 percent second of $40,000 at 8.5 percent is $307 a month. The total payment is $2,225 a month.
3. PMI—90 percent of first of $360,000 at 6.25 percent is $2,216 a month plus $160 PMI. The total payment is $2,376 a month.
4. The interest rate is higher because this is a 90 percent LTV ratio loan instead of the 80 percent piggyback.
5. Lender-paid PMI—There is no separate PMI premium because it is included in the rate. The 90 percent LTV ratio first loan's rate will be at 6.5 percent. The monthly payment is $2,275 a month.

You can see in this example that the piggyback payment is lower and that all the interest is tax deductible. PMI premiums are not tax deductible for your primary residence. Rates for the loans and premiums for PMI vary widely. Since every situation is unique, I sit down and price it out to see what makes the most sense. I get surprised all the time.

PMI premiums increase the less you put down. A PMI premium for a 100 percent financing can be close to 1 percent. To buy a $400,000 property with no money down, the PMI premium would be $400,000 × 1 percent = 4,000 yearly for a $333 monthly premium. Here is an example.

1. PMI: $400,000 T 6.5 percent (100 percent financing) = $2,528 principal and interest (PI) + $333 PMI = $2,861 a month
2. Piggyback: 80/20 (80 percent first, 20 percent second). Thus:
   - First: $320,000 × 6.5 percent = $2,022
   - Second: $80,000 × 9.0 percent = $643, for a total payment of $2,665 a month

Piggyback loans usually work out better for several reasons:

1. The interest is tax deductible.
2. They can be easier to get.
3. There can be a lower payment.

PMI has made it possible over the years for many people to qualify for low-down-payment loans. PMI loans do have their pluses, which include:

1. People can get PMI taken off later.
2. They can have a lower payment.
3. Borrowers do not have to take higher-interest-rate second mortgages.
4. In some situations, such loans may be all that are available.

PREPAYMENT PENALTIES: GOOD OR EVIL?

With the advent of the many innovative loan programs these days, pre-payment penalties have become more common. No longer are consumers restricted to the garden-variety 30- and 15-year fixed-rate programs. Interest-only loans, stated income loans, 3- and 5-year fixed-rate loans have brought to the marketplace more choice in the types of loan programs. Prepayment penalties have made many of these loans possible.

Are prepayment penalties bad? Not necessarily. They are a tool you can use to your advantage.

PREPAYMENT PENALTIES: WHAT ARE THEY AND WHAT DO THEY DO?

If you pay off the loan early in excess of 20 percent of the original loan amount, there is a financial penalty. Prepayment penalties benefit the lender because the lender knows that you are going to hold the loan longer. Loan companies offering an initially low interest rate most often will require prepayment penalties, particularly with adjustable-rate loans. They know that you are probably not going to sell or refinance quickly, so there is a built-in profit. The term for prepayment penalties can last for six months to as long as five years.

The amount of the penalty is figured two ways:

1. 6 months' interest on 80 percent of the original loan balance (more common)
2. 2 percent of the original loan balance

For an original loan balance of $320,000 at 6 percent interest, the prepayment penalty would be either (1) $15,360 or (2) $6,400.

The longer the prepayment penalties, the better rate you may get—possibly a 0.25 or 0.50 percent lower rate. Take a prepay if you are absolutely certain that you are not going to touch that loan by selling the house or refinancing the loan.

How do you not get a prepayment penalty? By refusing to even consider it, the loan companies will have to offer you other alternatives.

Most loan programs I have seen offer you a choice to buy out the pre-payment penalty to a lesser period of time or down to zero years. It will cost you anywhere from 0.25 to 1 point to do so. Some lenders will waive the prepay or at least lower it if you refinance the loan with them, a new buyer assumes the loan (and pays them an assumption fee), or the buyer takes out the purchase loan with them.

9

SHOULD I LOCK IN MY INTEREST RATE? TO LOCK OR NOT TO LOCK, THAT IS THE QUESTION

B orrowers always wonder if they should lock in interest rates when they first apply for a loan—or should they wait and see where the market goes. There is no sure answer because either choice involves some risk. If you lock now and rates fall, you lose, although some lenders may give you one free relock. If you don't lock now and rates rise, you also lose.

Alternatively—and here's the good news—you win by locking before rates rise, and you also win by not locking in a market where rates are falling.

How do interest-rate locks work, and when should I use them? Let's first consider how the Federal Reserve defines them:

A lock-in, also called a rate-lock or rate commitment, is a lender's promise to hold a certain interest rate and a certain number of points for you, usually for a specified period of time, while your loan application is processed. . . . A lock-in that is given when you apply for a loan may be useful because it's likely to take your lender several weeks or longer to prepare, document, and evaluate your loan application. During that time, the cost of mortgages may change. But if your interest rate and points are locked-in, you should be protected against increases while your application is processed. It is important to recognize that a lock-in is not the same as a loan commitment, although some loan commitments may contain a lock-in.

The most common lock-in periods are for 21, 30, 45, and 60 days. Some lock-in terms are longer for new construction when your property will not be finished for many months. The longer time period you lock in for, the more it costs. If you ask a lender to commit to an interest rate for an extended period of time, the lender will go to the secondary market and ask for what is called a *forward commitment.* You have reserved the interest rate for a defined period of time, and that costs the lender money.

There is usually no charge for the shorter-term locks. However, 30-day locks can cost ⅛ point, and 45- and 60-day locks can be ½ to ¾ point cost. Loan locks cost the lender money, so be sure that is what you want to do. Some lenders will require you pay the lock-in fee up front and probably will refund it at the end.

HOW CAN YOU MAKE SURE THAT YOU GET YOUR RATE?

There is no way to be 100 percent certain. Some lenders say that they lock in your rate, but they let it float and play the market so that they can

Because of these flaws, I never use APRs when shopping for my loans. The APR basically is useless. Instead, I want to know what the total cost is of the loan and the interest rate. Then I hold the lender to it.

Consumers need to know how to shop for loans. Although the initial intent of the TILA was to do just that, lenders have distorted and stretched the boundries of the law. Just know that buying property, using bank loans, and getting to the closing table can be a long, arduous, and frustrating adventure. In the next few pages, I will teach you how to anticipate in advance why loans don't close. It probably will cost you more and take longer than you expect—just like remodeling your house. There are lots of hands touching your real estate transactions, and they all need to be paid their reasonable charges.

You are remodeling your future by buying houses. Don't trip over the pennies to get at the dollars. Debt is a wonderful tool, rightly used.

make more money if rates go lower. If rates move the other way, they will lose money and probably find some excuse to delay the process. It has happened to me when I have used certain lenders for my loans.

Delays are common during the loan/purchase process, so if you lock in your rate, make very sure that you are going to close by the due date. There are a hundred ways that the closing can be delayed, some legitimate and some not, and I have seen them all. You lose your interest rate after that commitment period expires. Then you have to relock at the going rate. Some lenders will let you extend your rate lock, but it will cost you more. You can avoid delays with your lender by making sure that you are available at all times and by getting your paperwork in on time.

As a mortgage broker, I get a written loan commitment from my investor so that I can be sure that I don't get jerked around. I give a copy of that internal lock-in form to my borrowers to put them at ease.

If rates are stable, I usually float for a while, but not if rates are whipsawing around. In this way, if rates are in a momentary lull, I can take advantage of the dip.

WHAT IS AN APR, AND IS IT ANY GOOD? THE TRUTH ABOUT ANNUAL PERCENTAGE RATES
The Cost of Credit

The Truth-in-Lending Act (TILA) is a federal law that was enacted in order to better inform consumers on the cost of obtaining credit—car loans, mortgage loans, credit cards, and so on. Prior to TILA, lenders were under no legal requirement to make full disclosure of the terms of a loan. As a result, it was not uncommon for lenders to advertise loans with low interest rates but which included undisclosed fees and charges.

One of the key provisions of TILA was the requirement that a lender must disclose the *annual percentage rate* (APR) of the loan when the lender advertises an interest rate. Also, after you have applied for a mortgage loan, the lender must provide you a Truth-in-Lending Disclosure Statement that discloses the APR for your specific loan.

Calculation of the APR includes certain fees associated with a loan, thus informing consumers as to the "true" cost of the loan. In theory, a consumer should be able simply to compare the APRs offered by different lenders to determine which lender is offering the best deal.

Unfortunately, the APR is calculated in different ways using different fees. We will see the unreliability of strictly using an APR to pick the best loan, but first let's see how APRs are calculated.

APR Calculation

Remember John Q. Borrower's loan of $340,000? His 30-year fixed-rate loan was at 6 percent, and his payments were $2,083 a month. If he paid no points and had no loan fees, his APR also would be 6 percent. If he paid 1 point, the loan-origination fee would be $3,400. By paying $3,400, he is really receiving $336,600 (the $340,000 loan less the $3,400 fee). Under TILA, calculation of the APR is based on the net loan amount of $336,600, which means that his $2,083 monthly payment is cast over an effective loan amount of $336,600. The interest rate is still 6 percent, but his APR is 6.09 percent.

The problem with APR calculations is that not all fees are included in the calculations. The loan-origination fee is included, but title insurance is not. The appraisal fee may be included, but maybe not. Title insurance is not included by most lenders, but some include the escrow fee. And so on.

TILA does not provide a complete list of what fees must be included in the APR calculation but instead only provides a general overview. This means that each lender has some latitude to decide which fees to include in the APR. The result is that on the same loan different lenders can possibly calculate different APRs.

YOU ARE THE KINGMAKER OF THE TRANSACTION: HOW TO STAY IN CONTROL AND NOT GET RIPPED OFF

We all work for you. All of us—lenders, realtors, title reps, appraisers, and escrow agents—are in your employ. You need to realize that you have choices in the people you use. Hopefully, by reading this book, you are learning more about how loans work and how to make wiser financial choices.

KNOW YOUR OPTIONS

I cannot tell you how many times people have called me after their transaction was done and they got the wrong loan for their situation.

They say that they were not given more than one loan option. There are many loan options for every scenario.

You are not restricted to use a certain lender just because somebody tells you to. Call around and get several opinions about which loan program is best for you. Use real estate providers who have been recommended to you or use somebody you know who has been successful.

As you have seen, there are many loan options for every situation. The home loan explosion has given to the marketplace a huge variety of loan programs—stated income, no documentation (no doc), no income, no to low down payment, no asset adjustables based on all sorts of indices, short-term fixed loans that may or may not go interest-only, and 30-, 15-, and 10-year loans. All these loan programs have their pros and cons depending on your individual circumstances. The real estate providers you work with should explain all these options.

DEVELOP YOUR TEAM

Choosing the right people to work for you is crucial:

1. *Lenders.* You want somebody who has been in the business for a long time. A good loan officer can take care in advance of the most common problems that delay closing. Credit issues, lack of seasoned funds, properties not appraising at the stated value, debt-to-income ratios coming in too high, misquoting rates and costs, and not clearly understanding program requirements are the most common sources of confusion in the marketplace.

   In recent years, there has been a flood of new people entering the lending field. They may not fully understand what underwriters are looking for owing to their inexperience. Lenders may be too busy to call you back. If somebody ever says to me that he meant to call me but that he just got too busy, then he is too busy to work with me. That is not good.

2. *Realtors.* Has your realtor been referred to you from a trusted source? Successful realtors have to have a good record to last long in the business. Before using a new realtor, I usually call around and talk to her colleagues to verify what she has told me. Remember, realtors do not make any money unless they sell you their stuff.

   A good realtor is revealed by the people he or she refers to you. The caliber of people—title companies, property inspectors, and escrow and closing attorneys—who work with realtors speaks volumes.

3. *CPAs.* A good certified public accountant (CPA) can save you loads of money. I look for one who works with several investors and who owns real estate investments himself or herself. Knowing what you can and can't write off keeps money in your pocket and away from the tax auditor's table. CPAs are particularly helpful during 1031 tax-deferred exchanges.

ANTICIPATE IN ADVANCE WHY LOANS DON'T CLOSE

Have you ever wondered why your loan didn't go through? Did the points and interest rate you were quoted at first change mysteriously? Did you ever think that you had one kind of a loan only to have it change at the very end?

In a perfect world, this never should happen. With my clients, it seldom happens because I underwrite the loan upfront, and I know what my underwriters are looking for. I shudder when I hear some of the things that borrowers were told by other loan agents.

Even I have the occasional loan that does not close or the quoted terms change. Here are the 33 main reasons from the lender's perspective:

Lender

1. The borrower does not tell the truth on the loan application.
2. The borrower submits incorrect information to the lender.
3. The loan agent does not understand program guidelines.
4. The loan agent is inexperienced in this type of transaction.
5. The borrower has recent late payments on credit reports.
6. The lender found out about additional debt after the loan application.
7. The borrower loses his or her job.
8. The coborrower loses his or her job.
9. Verified income is lower than what was stated on the loan application.
10. Overtime income is not allowed by the underwriter for qualifying.
11. The applicant makes large purchase on credit before closing.
12. There is illness, injury, divorce, or another financial setback during escrow.
13. The borrower lacks motivation to go through the loan process or the purchase transaction.
14. The borrower cannot locate his or her divorce decree.
15. The borrower cannot locate his or her petition or discharge of bankruptcy.
16. The borrower cannot locate his or her tax returns.
17. The borrower cannot locate his or her bank statements.
18. There is difficulty in obtaining verification of rent.
19. The interest rate increases, and the borrower no longer qualifies.
20. The loan program changes with higher rates, points, and fees.
21. Child support paid out is not disclosed on application.
22. The borrower is a foreign national.
23. The borrower has had a bankruptcy within the last two years.
24. The mortgage payment is double the previous housing payment.

25. The borrower/coborrower does not have steady two-year employment history.
26. The borrower brings in handwritten pay stubs.
27. The borrower switches from a salary job to 100 percent commission income.
28. The borrower/coborrower/seller dies.
29. Family members or friends do not like what the home buyer chooses.
30. The buyer is too picky about property in a price range he or she can afford.
31. The buyer feels that the house was misrepresented.
32. The buyer has spent money needed for the down payment and closing costs and comes up short at closing.
33. The buyer does not properly "paper trail" additional money that comes from gifts, loans, and so on.

Again, make sure that you get your paperwork to the lender when he or she wants it and always be accessible to your lender, and your loan should close on time. Your loan documents will be at the same rate and will come in as quoted, and everything should be fine.

During a transaction, there are many things that can go wrong from the realtor's side. I have seen eight main things that have slowed or killed purchase transactions:

Realtor(s)

1. The realtor has no client control over buyers or sellers.
2. The realtor delays access to property for inspection and appraisals.
3. The realtor is unfamiliar with his or her client's financial position. Does the client have enough equity to sell?
4. The realtor does not get completed paperwork to the lender on time.

REAL ESTATE DEBT CAN MAKE YOU RICH

5. The realtor is inexperienced in this type of property transaction.
6. The realtor takes unexpected time off during the transaction and can't be reached.
7. The realtor jerks around other parties to the transaction. He or she has a huge ego.
8. The realtor does not do sufficient homework on his or her clients or on the property and wastes everyone's time.

BE A WISE LOAN CONSUMER

For the novice or very astute loan consumer, I give you Dexter's top five tips on getting a loan:

1. Never sign a contract without knowing and understanding the terms of your loan. When signing your loan documents, the two most important papers to pay attention to are the *note* (the official contract between you and the lender) and the *final closing statement* (HUD-1) from the closing agent, where all costs are finalized. Pay close attention to any document that has numbers on it.
2. Beware of door-to-door, Internet, or phone solicitations. If you did not seek them out, why are they seeking you out? Answer: More money for them.
3. Never allow yourself to be pressured into a loan. I always tell people what is going on upfront so that they know all their loan options and there are no surprises at the closing table.
4. Make sure that you can afford the proposed payments. Do not agree to payments you cannot make comfortably.
5. Only deal with real estate providers with whom you feel comfortable. Get referrals from your friends or from trusted real estate professionals.

2

USE YOUR DEBT WISELY: THE TOP 16 MISTAKES REAL ESTATE INVESTORS MAKE AND HOW TO AVOID THEM

I am a merchant of debt; I have been putting people in debt for 15 years. I know what to tell you because I mentor people all day about what are the best loans for them given their goals and aspirations.

At several colleges in southern California, where I teach my real estate classes, I asked over 4,000 students who had taken my seminars what they most wanted to hear regarding loans.

I structured this book based entirely and exactly on their feedback. And now I am going to give some guidance on the best ways I know to invest in real estate and how to avoid making the 16 biggest mistakes.

MISTAKE #1. NOT KNOWING WHAT YOUR PERSONAL GOALS ARE

- What is your exit strategy?
- You must ask yourself why you are buying this property.
- Set clear goals on exactly what you expect this property to do for you. Based on past performance, project into the future what this property will be doing for you 5, 10, and 25 years from now.
- How long will you hold on to the property?
- Do you intend to fix it up and resell it for a quick profit?
    1. If you do this, you usually have to buy 65 to 75 percent under market value to make any money.
    2. The buy, fix, and flip way to generate cash flow must be done carefully. Repair expenses and holding costs can eat into profits quickly.
- Real net worth is created by holding on to property long term and selling seldom. I would sell *if and only if:*
    1. Neighborhood quality is trending downward.
    2. There are *alligators*—rents that don't come close to your payment (too much negative cash flow is an alligator that can eat you alive).
    3. It is a home with a pool (if the tenants' little kid drowns, they're coming after you). Also, there are extra maintenance expenses.
    4. To pay off another property free and clear.
    5. You have tenant nightmares (easily resolved if you manage tenants the way I do).
    6. It is a condominium with escalating homeowner's association (HOA) assessments and an incompetent association.
    7. It will upgrade the quality of your real estate portfolio via 1031 tax-deferred exchanges.

- Holding on to property long term means that your rents will go up, principal is paid down, and market value increases. This results in equity expansion and higher net worth. You can use the positive cash flow to pay down the loan early or, if you are in the acquisition phase of your career, to purchase more investment properties.
- Here are some exit strategies:
  1. You can do a 1031 tax-deferred exchange. You can easily upgrade the quality of your real estate portfolio through tax-deferred exchanges into better houses.
     - Defer paying taxes and avoid depreciation recapture.
     - Increase the tax basis and get a greater depreciation deduction by acquiring property greater in value.
     - Change investment location into a better neighborhood.
  2. Buy or exchange into income property, that is, fourplexes, 10-plexes, and so on. You can live off the cash flow the rest of your life. Beware, though, of putting all your eggs in one basket, because in down markets apartments cut their rents first.
  3. Wait for your properties to appreciate, sell them all, pay the capital gains tax, and live off the proceeds. Move to a Caribbean island and sip umbrella drinks the rest of your life. *(Go to Jamaica, mon!)*
  4. Total positive cash flow. If you want to have 5 free and clear properties, buy 10 and then sell the worst and pay off the best.
     - Having 5 free and clear houses giving you $1,000 to $2,000 per month positive cash flow is wise. It is much easier to pay off your houses in big chunks with appreciated equity than applying small amounts monthly to your principal balance. For example, if you put an extra $200 a month into the principal, how long will it take to pay off the loan? Answer: Longer than selling an appreciated property and using the cash to retire debt.

5. Sell the property with creative financing techniques—lease option, installment sale, or land contract.

6. Carry back a note when you sell your property for a continuous stream of income. The new buyer can easily qualify if you wrap your existing loan with a new all-inclusive trust deed (AITD).

7. Do nothing. Let the tenant pay off your note in 20 to 30 years.

8. Rents will rise in that time.

9. Move into the property. Keep it or sell it (live in it for five years, and then you will pay no capital gains tax up to $250,000 if you are single or $500,000 if you are married).

- Are you buying the property for appreciation or cash flow? Lower-priced areas have better cash flows but may not go up much. At the same time, highly appreciating areas can have pretty hefty negative cash flows. How much cash flow are you willing to sacrifice for appreciation?

- It is cheaper to buy in lower-priced areas with higher cash flows, but do not be seduced by greater income because lower-end houses have:

1. Rent-collection problems.

2. Higher tenant wear and tear.

3. More maintenance calls.

4. More turnover. Tenants are transitory.

5. Less desirable neighborhoods.

6. More code enforcement violations, especially if the city is trying to upgrade the quality of the area.

- Stay away from war zones (high-crime-rate areas).

- At the opposite end of the spectrum, high-end houses located in attractive areas such as at the beach, near golf courses, and in mountain resorts generally appreciate well. However, these higher-level tenants tend to be helpless, demanding, and immature. They can skip out or know how to work the system, resulting in a prolonged eviction. Screen them carefully.

- The best and safest property to buy is in the low to middle range, where you can get acceptable appreciation without any significant negative cash flows. These areas attract upper-blue-collar types of tenants.
- Are you buying your property to enrich future generations?
  1. Heirs who inherit property often sell quickly because they are afraid to hang on to it and cannot manage tenants.
     - At probate sales, it is very common for property to be sold quickly at hefty discounts because the financial situation of the heir is so dire. Also, administrative costs and attorney fees can be very expensive.
  2. As long as the property is passed on via a living trust or a last will and testament, the heir will inherit a stepped-up basis (the current market value at death).
     - Do not put heirs on the title while you are still living because they will pay capital gains based on the original purchase price. They will lose their stepped-up basis status.

MISTAKE #2. NOT HAVING A BUYING SYSTEM IN PLACE

Do you have a buying system in place that gives you a continual source of leads? Where do find your deals? Here are 25 ways to buy properties. Pick just two or three of these buying systems and then become a master of them. Before long, you will have more deals than you know what to do with.

1. Buy out-of-state positive-cash-flow properties from Marshall Reddick at marshallreddickseminars.com.

2. Buy a run-down house at a discount with 100 percent financing, move in, and fix it up. Refinance and take out tax-free cash. Then rent it out and buy another one. Do it again.

3. Find a realtor who is used to working with investors and train him or her in exactly what you are looking for.

4. Newspaper classifieds. Find "For Sale by Owner" (FSBO) properties or well-priced listings with key words such as *owner transferred, divorce, motivated, owner financing possible,* and so on.

5. Advertise in both large- and small-circulation papers to have sellers call you.

6. Farming. Drive and become familiar with at least two neighborhoods you like. As you walk these areas, you will get to know the "mayor" of the block who knows everybody's business—who is moving, who is going broke, who has died, or who is getting a divorce.

7. Business cards. Give everyone you meet a card that says that you buy houses.

8. Bird dogs and finders—paper, pizza, and mail delivery people, meter readers, and so on. Hire somebody just to knock on doors.

113

9. Flyers. Post them everywhere you can, such as at selected farm areas, market bulletin boards, community bulletin boards, and laundries.

10. Signs. Create signs that say "I buy houses" and post them in high-traffic areas.

11. Public speaking. Become a name in the business, and you will get deals.

12. Foreclosures. Subscribe to a service such as www.foreclo sures.com. Call on or e-mail distressed homeowners as the listings come out, or go directly to the auction and bring cash, lots of it.

13. Bank foreclosures or REOs. Call to get on the list or look up the all-foreclosure.com Web site and call the listing agents.

14. Finance companies. Get to know the branch manager, and he or she can let you know who is in trouble. Look for companies such as Nationscredit, Avco, Beneficial, and The Associates.

15. Direct mail. Mail letters or postcards to owners of vacant or distressed-looking property.

16. Burnt-out landlords. Owners who have not been to my course get beaten up by their tenants. Get the eviction filings from the courthouse or direct mail to absentee owners in your area. Also, calling the "houses for rent" ads in your local newspaper can be an excellent source of leads.

17. Probate court. It will take some research to find out when the family will gets filed and who gets the property. Start with the obituary pages. After a few weeks, send a tasteful letter to the closest relative of the deceased inquiring if the property will be available for sale.

18. Divorce court. Divorce decrees are publicly recorded and often state that the property is to be sold and who gets the dough. Send a letter.

19. Vacant properties. Drive through neighborhoods and look for the tall weeds or the yellow lawns. Look up the owners in the public records. I have some friends who hire private detectives to come up with phone numbers.

20. Moving and yard sales. These sales can mean that somebody is moving.

21. Government. The VA, FHA, SBA, USDA, FDIC, and IRS all get properties back. Good Web sites are www.hud.gov/homes/homes forsale.cfm and www.all-foreclosure.com.

22. Attorneys. Attorneys often know when people need money to pay their fees. Keep your name in front of them because they know about deaths, divorces, and all sorts of tragedies that befall their clients.

23. Homebuilders. In slower markets, builders hate to get caught with excess inventory on hand, especially if it is one of the last remaining houses before they continue to their next phase.

24. Introduce yourself to the local building inspector and take him or her to lunch. Building inspectors have intimate knowledge of the neighborhood, know where all the fixer-uppers are, and know which owners are having trouble keeping up with repairs.

25. Get a real estate license. You will find the bargain properties when they become listed, and you can use your commission toward the down payment and closing costs. Better yet, option the seller's property at a lower price and sell it yourself at a higher price. You will make much more than a real estate agent's standard commission.

MISTAKE #3. NOT BEING AWARE OF ALL THE TYPES OF CREATIVE FINANCING

- You can be out of the game before you start if you do not take good care of your credit. If you do not have good credit and income to qualify for conventional loans, you will need cleverness and skill to structure deals creatively or a partner with good credit and income or who has cash.

- Be aware of unconventional loan sources. There are institutional and private lenders who lend "hard money" based solely on a property's equity and not on your income and credit.

- If you find a deal that is sweet enough, you do not need good credit or income; the money will come to you.

- What you lack in income and credit you must make up for with creativity and cunning.

- Financing creates value. Many times creative owner-financing can leave conventional loans in the dust. Your ability to negotiate favorable terms can leave owner's equity on the sidelines and can make the difference between a negative and positive cash flow.

- Do you know how to talk directly with an owner and devise a creative financing strategy that he or she will understand, will meet his or her needs, and will create a win-win situation for both of you?

- Do you know anybody with a lot of money sitting in a low-yielding investment? Real estate can offer such a wealthy individual a great return on his capital, and you can fuel your real estate ventures without going to the bank.

MISTAKE #4. NOT HAVING ADEQUATE CASH RESERVES AND NOT MANAGING DEBT RESPONSIBLY

- Not being able to handle unforeseen vacancies and maintenance and overleveraging is the number one reason real estate investors go out of business. Many a budding real estate entrepreneur's career is over before it starts because he or she underestimated initial vacancies and maintenance and could not pay the loans. Too much debt can take your financial life.
  - What are you going to do if you close on a property one day and have to replace a $3,000 air conditioner the next?
  - Can you withstand the property not renting quickly?
- At least three months' payments of liquid cash per property should be retained; six months is recommended.
- You will run out of money before you run out of deals. Then you must get creative or get a partner.
- If you are going to buy and hold multiple single-family homes, does the idea of being millions of dollars in debt scare you? It shouldn't. The main thing to focus on is:
  1. Will your property rent easily?
  2. How quickly will it rent, and for how much?
- If times turn soft, can you cut your rents several hundred dollars a month and still be okay?
  - Buying well-located houses in high-demand neighborhoods eliminates the most risk in all of real estate. In down markets and up markets, there always will be people wanting to rent your house.
- Do you have the ability to refinance and pull cash out if you need to buy more houses?
- How about a line of credit? It is much easier to have a credit line when you do not need it than to try to get one when you really need one.

MISTAKE #5. NOT PAYING ATTENTION TO THE NUMBERS: EVERY PROPERTY HAS A DIFFERENT RETURN ON THE MONEY YOU PUT INTO IT

- What are the benefits according to cash flow, appreciation, depreciation, and amortization?
- There are four areas of profit potential:
  1. Appreciation
  2. Cash flow
  3. Depreciation
  4. Amortization
- Let's say that you bought a rental house for $210,000 at 10 percent down, paying 7 percent interest. The house was a foreclosure in bad shape, so it cost you another $12,000 to fix it up.
  - *Appreciation* is the gain in value of your investment. If the yearly appreciation rate in your area is 10 percent, then your $210,000 house will be worth $21,000 more next year.
  - *Cash flow* is the amount of cash left over after you pay your loan payment (PITI). The loan payment would be $1,460 monthly. The rents total $1,595 a month, making for a $135 a month positive cash flow.
  - *Depreciation* is the amount the IRS allows you to deduct from the building value each year multiplied by your tax bracket. In every purchase, the building value is usually 80 percent of the total purchase price. The rest is lot value. In this case, the building value is $168,000. The IRS says that the building has a useful life of 27½ years, or a factor of 3.64 percent. Thus $168,000 × 3.64 percent is $6,115 total depreciation. Multiply this by your tax bracket (37 percent, for example), and the net tax benefit to you is $2,262.

- *Amortization* is the amount your loan principal goes down each year. You need an amortization table or a financial calculator to do this. In this example the loan went down $1,919.
- Let's add up how much money you have made and figure your return on your investment.

Appreciation	$21,000
Cash flow	$ 1,620
Depreciation	$ 2,262
Amortization	$ 1,919
Total benefit	$26,801

- Remember, you spent $33,000 on your house in down payment and fix-up.

Money in	$33,000
Benefit out	$26,801

- Divide your money in into your benefit out, and you have just received a yield of 81 percent every year.
- Do you have any other investments giving you an 81 percent annual return?

Owning Real Estate Is Messy

These projected returns are never exact. I have many clients trying to project specific returns by using specific pro-formas or spreadsheets. Those pro-formas become out of date the minute the client buys the property because everything changes. Rents may not be what you thought, tenants may vacate unexpectedly, there may be more repairs or fix-up costs than anticipated, a crack house may suddenly appear next door, or the area may appreciate more or less in the future.

Real estate wealth accumulation is not a perfectly straight line, but the path is safe and certain. Your real estate success can be a tried-and-true road if you listen to others who have traveled it before you.

MISTAKE #6. NOT KNOWING
THE EXACT APPRECIATION RATE
FOR YOUR NEIGHBORHOOD

- You should know how much your property has gone up in the last three to five years and what the projected value will be in three to five years.
- Talking to the local board of realtors, you can find out the history of the area.
- What are reasons for the appreciation?
- Are jobs being created in the area, and are more people moving there? What is the surrounding industry?
- Job growth and population inflow determine the economic viability of an area. What is the economic engine that makes the area so attractive that people would want to buy and rent houses? (Appendix 1 lists economic Web sites.)

MISTAKE #7. NOT KNOWING
THE TOP 33 SIGNS THAT A NEIGHBORHOOD
IS GOING DOWNHILL OR IMPROVING

- Every neighborhood gentrifies over time, and older neighborhoods can be magnets for crime, delinquency, and drug problems. It is extremely important to identify neighborhood trends. Watch out if you see:

    1. Yards not being kept up.
    2. Businesses going under with vacant storefronts.
    3. Houses in a state of disrepair.
    4. Cars parked in yards.
    5. Deteriorating fences.
    6. More pawnshops and paycheck-cashing places than banks.
    7. Grocery store carts.
    8. Congested on-street parking with lots of grease spots.
    9. A large number of rental houses.

- Every neighborhood has a life cycle called *gentrification*. It is how the neighborhood ages itself. The neighborhood can stay the same, deteriorate and go downhill, or improve in value. This improvement is called *resurgence*. Signs that a neighborhood is resurging include:

    10. The neighborhood is starting to look better.
    11. New people are moving in.
    12. Older homes are being fixed up or torn down.
    13. A rise in owner occupants.
    14. Younger families walking the sidewalks with dogs and baby strollers.
    15. Banks and franchises moving in.
    16. New businesses being started.

17. Operations such as Home Depot, Lowe's, Starbucks, Blockbuster Video, Hollywood Video, Kohl's, Bed, Bath and Beyond, Barnes and Noble/Borders bookstores, high-end restaurants with outdoor seating, florists, clothing boutiques, upscale neighborhood malls with pedestrian walkways and bubbling fountains, and multiscreen entertainment megaplexes are moving in.

18. A good mix of resident-serving businesses—mom and pop stores and general stores—will attract regional/national chain enterprises.

- Outside factors that initiate resurgence include:

19. City declaring an area a historical district.

20. Relocation of a major employment center.

21. Increased transportation opportunities.

22. Rise in school scores.

23. City planners planning new improvements or upgrading infrastructure.

24. Government infusion of cash to upgrade neighborhoods.

25. Community redevelopment block grants to blighted areas.

26. Older inner-city areas getting rediscovered as suburbs get too expensive.

27. The local municipality forming a redevelopment district to attract commercial/residential development money.

28. Rezoning or downsizing population density.

29. Cities razing older apartment buildings and/or older business districts that were magnets for crime, delinquency, and drugs.

30. Stricter enforcement of building codes forcing owners to upgrade their buildings.

31. Increasing police visibility with more patrols and/or a police substation.

32. Neighborhood Watch committees forming.

33. More community involvement by service clubs (Lions Club or Rotary Club) or church ministries.

MISTAKE #8. NOT KNOWING THE EXACT RENTAL APPRECIATION RATE OF THE NEIGHBORHOOD

- Are rents going up or down? Why? What is the source of rental demand?
- Is there a lot of new construction in the area, oversupplying the market, which drives down rents?
- Is your property located close to multiunit housing? High-density apartments can detract from the area and depress rents.
- There should be a number put out by the local board of realtors that will tell you if the vacancy rate is the same, up, or down.
- Talk to active property managers in the area. They are on the front lines and can tell you vacancy rates, rental amounts, and lag times. They also will have a good view to the overall economic trends in the area.

MISTAKE #9. NOT HAVING PROPERTY IN RENT-READY CONDITION QUICKLY ENOUGH

- Every day that passes without rent is a negative-income day. You want as few of these days as possible.
- The property should be fixed up and attractively landscaped.
- Concentrate on the outside of the house and the front lawn first before getting started on the inside of the house.
  - When prospective tenants drive by your property, the lawn should be green and freshly mowed, shrubs and bushes neatly trimmed, and all junk and debris cleared away.
  - Get to know the neighbors, and you also will know which families have teenage sons or daughters who would be happy to mow the front lawn.
- Get gardeners over to the house for a few estimates, Usually you have to wait a day or two or more to get them to look at your lawn. This is wasted time! Every car that drives by your house with your large "For Rent" sign will stop, and if the lawn looks unkempt, they will drive on. If it's neat and tidy, they will write down your phone number or, better yet, come in and inquire about the rental.
- Do the exterior first. Even if the house needs paint on the inside and other items fixed or repaired on the interior, do the outside first because that is what prospective tenants see first. If someone really likes your house and wants to rent it, you conceivably could finish the minor interior items while they are living there. In that way, you don't lose any rental time while fixing up your property.
- You can even put new roofs on and install large air-conditioning units while the property is occupied. Tenants usually don't mind because they are going to benefit from these improvements.

- Call the utility companies to come out and check the heaters, air conditioners, and other appliances to make sure that they're safe and operating. This beats hiring a contractor or paying service calls to appliance companies for inspections. The gas company will come out for free and check the heater, water heater, and so on, and tell you what is wrong with it. Sometimes I do this while I'm still in escrow, and this really helps me get a head start on any work that needs to be done. Be very certain that the house will soon be yours.

- Accumulate lists of reliable handymen, painters, and other resources. Share these lists with other landlords, and they will share who they have with you. This may not seem important if you don't manage your own properties, but if you let someone else do the managing for you, your expense ratio will be approximately 30 to 35 percent higher.

- If you buy foreclosures or fixer-uppers, they are being sold "As Is" and have been neglected or abused for a long time. You may not know if the major systems in the houses are operative, especially if the utilities have been shut off.

- If you use contractors to tell you what "needs" to be done to your house before it can be rented, watch out—watch the costs grow. They'll have you ripping out cabinets and countertops and replacing all sorts of stuff that doesn't need to be replaced. You're not selling the house; you're renting it. Maybe those cabinets just need to be sanded and painted. You don't need granite countertops in a rental property. You'll still be able to rent the property for a nice sum with "regular" generic vanilla cabinets, flooring, and countertops.

- Have the property attractively landscaped. Placing fresh flowers in self-watering vases and scattering fresh-smelling potpourri around the house can improve the look and smell of your property dramatically. And these things don't cost much. If the house has an unpleasant odor that you can't get rid of by cleaning the carpet and scrubbing the walls, buy plug-in room deodorizers at the store. They work really well, especially if you open all the doors and air out the home.

Hold Tenant Open Houses: Rent Your House in One Day

- To get tenants quickly and inexpensively, have the tenants come to you! You will not waste time trying to show your house to prospects who never show up.
  - List your property with all free landlord services, and tell the callers that you will be there Sunday between one and five.
  - Put open house signs all around the neighborhood with directional arrows to create traffic.
  - Place flyers in close by retail establishments.
  - Put balloons or flags outside to attract attention.
  - Go to realtors holding open houses the same day. Tell them that you will send people wanting to buy if they will send people wanting to rent.
  - Go to area churches and place notices on their community bulletin boards.
  - Schools. If the property is near a school, call the student housing department.
  - Neighbors. Walk around the neighborhood and let the neighbors know that they have a chance to pick their neighbors.
- The quicker the house is freshly painted and smelling good, the quicker you will attract a quality tenant.
- During the month of December, I had five vacancies! Five vacancies during Christmas time is a cause for great landlord anxiety. I cut short my Christmas festivities and had all of them rented by

January 1. When you manage the property yourself, you don't mess around.

- Professional property managers who have other vacancies besides yours will not rent them as fast as you will. If the property has to be managed professionally, call the manager often to make sure that the property is rent-ready, being advertised, and being shown. Cut the rents if there is slow activity in the first two weeks.
- Make sure that quoted fix-up costs are reasonable to the area. Definitely look closely at the estimated fix-up costs because they can easily spiral out of sight.
- You should know what the local rate is for carpet, paint, and handywork. Get at least two or three estimates from everyone.
- If you are buying the house, start this process before you close on the house so that you can have the workers lined up to start work the day the purchase transaction closes.
- When you first purchase your property and it requires fix-up, make sure that you have the "right" things wrong with the property.
- Fresh paint, clean carpet, and minor handywork should be all that is required unless you know it to be a major fixer-upper.
- Painting is the least expensive way to change the look of a room and make it more appealing.
- Replacing old and/or dated kitchen cabinet knobs and adding new contemporary kitchen hardware updates the look in the kitchen. This is a very cheap improvement.
- Freshen up the look of the kitchen by adding inexpensive, colorful kitchen curtains found at Target or JCPenney's.
- Sometimes, when you're purchasing a foreclosure property that has been neglected or sitting vacant for a while, the roof will leak. Make sure that you figure the cost of fixing that item into your purchase price. Sometimes you can negotiate with the bank or the seller to get them to knock a couple of thousand dollars from the price if you can convince them the roof needs replacing.

■ On one house, I obtained a "certified" report from a roofing contractor that said that the roof was leaking and needed to be replaced. I gave this to the bank that held the REO property, and it deducted that amount from the purchase price.

• Air-conditioning units that sit on top of the roof will always leak. Make sure that the installation is done professionally, and get a good warranty. Every time it rains, the roof leaks where the A/C unit usually is.

MISTAKE #10. NOT KNOWING THE SURROUNDING NEIGHBORHOOD WELL

- Is your property close to noisy/heavily trafficked commercial areas?
- Is it under the flight path of a nearby airport?
- Is it across the street from a church or school, which can cause crowding and congestion? You will have a traffic jam twice a day with schools and on weekends with churches.
- Is the property very close to railroad tracks?
- If railroad tracks are nearby, how close is your property to a whistle stop? Check any nearby railroad crossings at different times of the day, because frequent whistle blasts can be very unsettling.
- Is it adjacent to a brightly lit commercial shopping center?
- Are you next to multiunit housing that can have marginal tenants, higher crime, and lower rents to compete with?
    - Cities zone high-density housing on the outskirts of residential neighborhoods. They transition the neighborhood use from residential to commercial.
- If you are buying in a new housing tract with lots of vacant land around, the neighborhood has yet to establish itself. In the future, the tract could be surrounded by higher-end housing or by high-density/commercial establishments. You can check with the local planning department to see what kind of development is planned next door. Nobody wants to live in an increasingly congested area with worsening traffic.
- Have you contacted the public information officer at the local police department to get call reports? The police can give you the number and type of criminal activity in your area.
- Have you gone to the city building department and pulled the file on your house to see if all additions and improvements have been permitted?

- Have you introduced yourself to the local building inspector? The longer the building inspector has been in your area, the better. Building inspectors know everything about the history of the house and the neighborhood.

Good Neighbors Can Make Remote Property Management Possible

- Get to know your neighbors well. They can be your eyes and ears and can call you if anything goes wrong. They also can show the property for you if you can't drive over there each time a tenant wants to see it.
  - You are upsetting the balance of the neighborhood by throwing renters at them. Quickly dispel their anxieties by letting them know that you intend to rent to people just like them and asking them if they know anybody who would rent your fine house. Tell them that you expect a very high standard of cleanliness and nondisruptive behavior from your tenants.
  - Let them know that their approval of the new tenant is important to you. Introduce your neighbors to the new tenant.

MISTAKE #11. NOT CARRYING ADEQUATE INSURANCE AND EXERCISING OTHER MEASURES TO PROTECT YOUR ASSETS

- Read your policy and know the limits of coverage.
- If you are renting out your residence, make sure that you get a landlord policy to cover any tenant liabilities.
- Make sure to periodically review your coverage and increase the dwelling coverage amount. Increasing liability coverage to the limit is cheap protection.
- Make sure that the tenants have renter's insurance in case of fire.
- Having umbrella insurance can protect you against dog bite lawsuits or if the tenants hurt themselves on your property.
- Privacy of ownership is important. Anything to disguise your ownership is wise. People cannot sue you if they cannot find you.
- The ideal is to control everything and appear to own nothing.
- Check out the pros and cons of how you hold title to your property. Look at whether a title-holding trust, a corporation, a partnership, or an LLC is best for you.

MISTAKE #12. NOT SCREENING TENANTS THOROUGHLY ENOUGH

- There are no bad tenants, just lazy landlords who failed to check a prospect out thoroughly.
- Not being able to effectively handle tenants is the number two reason real estate investors go out of business.
- The two times landlords get in trouble is when they are in a hurry or when they feel sorry for someone.
- If you choose to hold a renters' open house, have everybody come to you instead of you to them. Create interest, put open house signs around the neighborhood, and tell the neighbors. Tell everybody to come between noon and three or between one and four on a weekend. In this way, you have lots of people milling around in the house, creating energy and value.
- People residing in apartments are used to calling the landlord whenever anything breaks (and they break things more often). The tenant you select needs to know that houses do not run themselves and that he or she needs to be proactive when it comes to repairs.
- Know why your prospective tenant is moving and check out his or her story. Did the person get kicked out or leave the previous place on unpleasant terms?
- Has the applicant ever withheld rent because a landlord did not make a timely repair? If so, this is not a good sign.
- Beware of applicants who have a sense of entitlement. If they start nitpicking your place apart at the start, their attitude will not improve.
- Did you verify landlord references for the last five years? Make sure that you go beyond the most recent landlord because he or she may give a good reference just to get rid of the tenant.
- Does the present employer speak about the applicant in favorable terms and paint a positive picture about his or her future?

- Tenants getting fired in the middle of their leases become evictions.
- Total monthly household income must be three times monthly rent. You can consider all types of alternative income only if it is steady and is expected to last into the foreseeable future.
- Did you document what the applicant says he or she makes with tax returns, pay stubs, and bank statements? Qualifying to rent your house is like qualifying for a loan.
- Look up the applicant's employer in the phone book and look for a different address and phone number. If it is different, the applicant may be lying and having a friend verify employment.
- Also, on your rental application, ask for personal references as well as for phone numbers of relatives. Don't let applicants leave blank lines on the application. Check it over after the applicant is finished filling it out and make sure that he or she has answered all your questions.
- Visit the applicant's present domicile. How the house looks now will be how your house will look in the future. The same thing goes for the applicant's car.
- Ask to see the applicant's driver's license to prove his or her identity.
- Do you have a multipage lease agreement that states in clear and understandable language what you expect from the applicant?
- Spend at least an hour or two with the applicant when writing the lease. Lay down the house rules so that there is no doubt about what you expect from the applicant.
- The first 30 to 60 days is crucial in the relationship. Tenants will test you. Will you train them or will they train you?
- There is no grace period for late payment. Let your tenant know in no uncertain terms that if the rent is not received on the due date there is an immediate late charge and eviction proceedings are imminent.

- Have a post office box or mail drop to receive the rent. No need to have an irate or vengeful tenant darkening your door.
- Get extra deposit money and/or a cosigner if a prospect is marginal.
- If you do get a tenant who stops paying the rent, don't just serve an eviction notice. Call the tenant up, ask what happened, and if he or she can get the money from a parent, friend, or relative. Call the tenant's church and talk to the pastor.
- Ask for an emergency phone number on the application. This is the number you call when the rent doesn't come in!
- Staple a smoke alarm disclosure to your lease agreement. Photograph or videotape the locations of the alarms. This is most helpful in court if the property burns.
- Make sure that the tenant signs a drug-free addendum. Having friends over for drinks is fine, but if they are caught with anything stronger, the tenant is out.
- If you take pets, the dog pays doggy rent.
- Insist on initial rent and security deposit by cashiers check only; thereafter personal checks are fine until the tenant bounces one on you. Take only certified funds after that.
- Good tenant management is simply managing people. Screen tenants the best you can according to credit, bounced checks, and previous evictions. Check their stories, see if their employers like them, and look them straight in the eye. Tenants need to know that you are not their friend, babysitter, parent, or banker. You are their *boss*, and they are valued employees. They have four jobs to do:

1. Pay the rent on time.
2. Be a good steward of the asset.
3. Get along with the neighbors.
4. Leave you alone.

- The better you are at managing the relationship, the more successful you will be.

MISTAKE #13. NOT DOUBLE-CHECKING THE SELLER OR HIS OR HER AGENT'S FINANCIAL NUMBERS BECAUSE YOU GET CAUGHT UP IN THE EXCITEMENT

- *Claims of extremely high rates of returns are rampant in real estate investment.* Have you cross-checked the projected rent, appreciation, and vacancy rate? Is the rental market strong or soft in the given area? Verify, verify, and then verify some more.

- Don't take for granted any answers that you get. Remember, salespeople can't stay in business unless they sell you their stuff. Thus, take what they say with a grain of salt.
- My wife once bought a house in Sherman Oaks, south of Ventura Boulevard, and the realtor actually told her that airplanes aren't allowed to fly over that area!
- Another investor had a real estate agent tell him that no property inspection is needed for properties sold in probate court. Later, he found out that the only thing holding the house together was all the termites holding hands!

MISTAKE #14. NOT INSPECTING YOUR PROPERTY THOROUGHLY

- Are you getting to know the property you have bought? Unless you are a contractor with intimate knowledge of house construction, hire a reputable licensed property inspector. Follow him or her around and ask lots of questions.
- Hire one *not* recommended by the seller or his or her agent. An in-house inspector owes his or her business (and allegiance) to the seller, so he or she may not be as forthcoming about material defects. Look for an inspector licensed by the American Society of Home Inspectors (ASHI); this association has tough membership requirements (www.ashi.com).
- New houses need professional inspection because builder defects are common.
- Bring a clipboard and have a preassigned list of questions for the inspector. When he or she is done with the inspections, sit down and discuss each item of concern.
- Good inspectors are only too happy to explain the defects they uncover.
- Have you devised an inspection checklist that you can use for each house that you buy?
- One of the best ways to find the best inspector available is to find the best real estate agent in the area (with no vested interest in your transaction) and ask who he or she would use when buying a personal residence.
- Ask the tenants and the neighbors about pest and insect problems, structural damage, or recurring problems. Don't overlook anything!

MISTAKE #15. NOT ACQUIRING
ADDITIONAL INCOME-PRODUCING ASSETS

- Upgrading and improving your property are very good things to do. Especially in times of high property values and low property acquisition, putting money back into your investment is wise.
- Buying high-yielding houses is the highest and best use of your money.
- Many successful investors have free and clear properties. Rapidly paying down your loan (hopefully with appreciated equity and not after-tax dollars) decreases your debt load and increases your equity, which builds your net worth.
- In the end—especially if you are buying your first investment property—just go out and buy a house. It doesn't have to be a killer deal or carry fancy seller financing. Just jump in and do it. Follow as many of the rules I have outlined as you can, and you will be fine. I will repeat five of the most important ones:

1. Buy a well-located single family house in a high demand neighborhood where people want to be, need to be, and *have* to be.

2. Find out what industries are in your town and what the potential for job growth is. Astute investors become amateur economists and know well where their tenants work and how much they make. Property owners who have houses to receive the surge of job-seekers flooding these areas will get an enduring and durable supply of renters.

3. Buy investment-grade property priced below the median house price for your area. If you stick with a three-bed two-bath house sized at 1,000–1,600 square feet in the growth path of your town, you have just bought the most in-demand piece of real estate in the country.

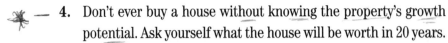

4. Don't ever buy a house without knowing the property's growth potential. Ask yourself what the house will be worth in 20 years.

5. Remember, responsible use of debt is a pillar of building wealth.

MISTAKE #16. NOT REMEMBERING THAT YOU ARE BUYING A BUSINESS THAT REQUIRES YOU TO THINK AND ACT DIFFERENTLY

- Are you ready to treat your investment activities as a business, keeping track of your income and expenses? Real estate is not "hands off" and requires your active participation.
- Owning investment property carries with it a great potential for wealth—and tough decisions. Managing your time, dealing with your tenants, handling repairs and evictions, and learning landlord-tenant law are essential to being successful in this business.
- Are you going to additional real estate seminars on a regular basis? Dedicating at least 10 percent of your time, money, and talent to learning new strategies and networking with other investors will ensure your success.
- Network with other landlords at real estate seminars, workshops, and meetings. As you start to own more and more property, you'll find out how very valuable it is to be able to pick up the phone to call fellow landlords and ask who it is they call when their roofs leak or their pipes leak from old age.
- You must have a buying system in place to give you a continual source of leads. Where will you find your deals?
- The following 10 guidelines work in the investment business and in life:
  1. How you think is everything.
  2. Decide on your true dreams and goals. Real estate is a means to an end. What is your reward? The clearer you can see your reward, the more it will compel you to move forward. This is especially useful during the tough times.
  3. Take action. Do not be a professional seminar taker.

4. Never stop learning. There is always somebody ahead of you who knows more than you. And there is somebody following you whom you must teach.

5. Be persistent and work hard. If you are young and hungry, this may be all you have to offer.

6. Learn to analyze details. Knowing how to crunch numbers is more attractive when they have dollars attached to them.

7. Focus your time and money. The less time you waste, the more efficient you are, and the quicker you hit your goals.

8. Be different. Successful real estate investors are a varied lot, and they don't hesitate to find their own niches. March to the beat of the different drummer because financial success gives you the freedom to do so. Don't hesitate to do things your own way.

9. Deal and communicate with people effectively. If you can get tenants to obey your rules and at the same time have a good reputation with your fellow investors, you are halfway home.

10. Take responsibility. You make your investment decisions based on the information you find. If things do not turn out the way you want, there is nobody to blame but yourself. The keys to success are within you or can be discovered readily.

LIST OF RESOURCES

1. *www.richdebt.com.* My Web site will be very useful if you want to use the principles in this book.

2. *www.homesales.gov.* I have bought 11 houses because of this information! Foreclosed homes for sale from the U.S. government. They are from the U.S. Department's of Housing and Urban Development (HUD), the Veteran's Administration (VA), Agriculture (USDA), and the Small Business Administration (SBA).

3. *www.realtytimes.com.* This free Web site is a repository for realtor newsletters nationwide. It is a great source for local knowledge in a specific neighborhood. Although realtors are salespeople and their newsletters can be a bit fluffy, there is no substitute for having somebody "on the ground" with whom you cross-check information.

4. *www.realtor.org.* Click on the research bar and get the appreciation rates for the top 100 metropolitan areas nationwide!

5. *www.ofheo.gov.* Office of Federal Housing Enterprise Oversight—great research site—gives housing prices and appreciation rates for states and most major metropolitan areas.

6. *www.cnnmoney.com.* This one-stop Web site has it all! Very current business information and a very complete real estate news site.

7. *www.zillow.com.* To check the value of almost any property in the nation, you get a satellite map of your property and the sales prices of all other houses on the block.

8. *www.inmannews.com.* Paid subscriber site that gives very good daily real estate news.

9. *www.newspapers.com.* Access the nation's newspapers online. Scan the daily business pages for updated economic information.

10. *www.realestatejournal.com.* Brought to you by the folks at the *Wall Street Journal.* Learn about the current real estate/business environment.

Find Out about Foreclosures and Bank Repos Near You

11. *www.all-foreclosure.com.* One of the best sites for REOs and government foreclosures. Not only does it have extensive information about how foreclosures work, it has actual bank repos listed for sale. I bought three as the result of finding this site.

12. *www.foreclosureforum.com.* San Diego–based foreclosure specialist. Good chat room and free sample grant deeds, lease agreements, notes, and purchase contracts. Very informative on how foreclosures work.

13. *www.foreclosures.com.* Tells about foreclosure procedures in each state and also has a service that will track foreclosures in most areas.
14. *www.realtytrac.com.*

Locate Investment Property Nationwide and Find Out How Much It Is Worth

15. *www.realtor.com.* This National Association of Realtors Web site gets you in contact with member realtors and their listings. Find contractors, movers, and local real estate vendors. Good background resources.
16. *www.dqnews.com.* Data Quick's Web site has very current information regarding changes in median home prices. It covers all metropolitan areas in California and 10 other states.
17. *www.homegain.com.* Find a home or realtor, home valuations, and online comparables. You will have to supply some personal information, though.
18. *www.ziprealty.com.* Online comparables. Personal information required.
19. *www.homeradar.com.* Good articles and online comparables.
20. *www.ebayrealestate@ebay.com.* This Web site will e-mail you sales as they happen in any area.
21. *www.truiia.com.* Has a nationwide database of varied listings in all areas. Easy to use.

Great Places to Find Out about Job Growth and Where People Are Moving

22. *www.fedstats.gov.* Great Web site for you data dogs out there. You can find out where people work, how much they make, and how many live in a given area.

23. *www.bls.gov.* From the U.S. Bureau of Labor Statistics, this very huge and voluminous database is for serious data dogs only!

24. *www.bea.gov.* This Web site summarizes the complex data from the BLS data above. It gives a nice synopsis of all states' most recent unemployment data, personal income growth, types of industries, and current area GDPs.

25. *www.census.gov.* From the U.S. Census Bureau Web site, you can find out the cost of living (CPI) in any area, the types of industries, and vacancy rates. Demographic and economic data and much more!

26. *www.chamberofcommerce.com.* Access local economic information from the group most responsible for promoting the area's business interests.

27. *www.bestplaces.net.* All criteria—best appreciation, lowest home prices, best schools, lowest crime, etc.

28. *www.reef.com.* This is a paid subscriber site, but it has a free terrific economic map that graphically displays U.S. economic activity state by state.

Other Commentators on the Real Estate Scene Nationwide

29. *www.localmarketmonitor.com.* A very good survey for future economic trends in over a 100 different metropolitan areas. Somewhat dated but has enough free information to be useful.

30. *www.erc.org.* Future job growth in different areas of the country. What makes this site unique is that it surveys human resources professionals who do the actual hiring for major corporations. When and where they hire, how

many jobs they will have, and how much they will pay is vital information.

Free Property Profiles Are Worth the Money

31. *www.titleadvantage.com.* Run your own property profiles and sales comparables for free. This is the same as having your own account at a title company.

Your Credit: How to Find Out about Your Credit Score and Repair It

32. *www.myfico.com.* Get your credit score online and a copy of your credit report from this secure site. Best Web site to get the straight scoop on how they compute credit scores straight from the horse's mouth, the Fair Isaac Company.

33. *www.equifax.com.* Order your credit report from one of the big three agencies.

34. *www.transunion.com.* Order your credit report from one of the big three agencies.

35. *www.experian.com.* Order your credit report from one of the big three agencies.

36. *www.creditinfocenter.com.* Lots of free information revealing credit scores and how to repair credit. Highly recommended.

37. *www.mortgage-investments.com.* A great resource for owner direct financing. Read this before you start negotiating with sellers.

38. *www.bankrate.com.* Well-regarded Web site gives loads of information about how credit works, credit cards for people with poor credit, how to complain to credit bureaus, and much, much more.

39. *www.mortgage101.com.* Beginner's guide to mortgages.

Learn about Local, National, and International Business and Economic Trends

40. *www.money.com.* Recommended reading for general financial news.

41. *www.yahoo.com.* Yahoo.com.finance.

42. *www.fortune.com.* Recommended reading for general financial news.

43. *www.forbes.com.* Recommended reading for general financial news.

44. *www.economist.com.* Find out what is happening globally.

45. *www.ita.doc.gov.* This International Trade Association site gives oodles of trade and export data from all states and the United States to show international trade activity. Very important information that reveals that no place is isolated in our growing global village.

My Best Gurus, Where You Will Get the Best Knowledge Without Paying an Arm and a Leg

46. *www.bobbruss.com.* Bob Bruss is a very knowledgeable real estate investor and attorney who writes a weekly real estate column for the major newspapers. Publishes a very consumer-friendly newsletter.

47. *www.cashflowconcepts.com.* Long one of the brightest minds in the creative real estate business, Jack Miller has done it better and longer than most and writes a great newsletter.

48. *www.davidtilney.com.* Everything you need to know about managing the tenant-landlord relationship. My property management guru.

49. *www.johnschaub.com.* John will teach you everything you need to know about the house business. Very good teacher.

50. *www.peterfortunato.com.* Peter Fortunato has a very informative style that focuses on people, documentation, and negotiation. His paper course set a standard in the industry.

51. *www.louisbrown.com.* Louis Brown has the best and most complete paperwork in the business. A knowledgeable and down-to-earth investor/teacher. Somewhat more expensive but worth the money.

52. *www.marshallreddickseminars.com.* One of my first and best gurus, Marshall does a lot of economic research to buy properties in all the best areas nationwide.

Gurus I Have Heard About

53. *www.adkessler.net.* A. D. Kessler, publisher of *Creative Real Estate* magazine.

54. *www.zick.net.* Barney Zick, specializing in real estate options and negotiations.

55. *www.bestrealestatesite.net.* Information materials run by Mark Walters.

56. *www.claudediamond.com.* Claude Diamond, mentor services, great information about lease options.

57. *www.creonline.com.* Creative Real Estate Online. Many free and informative articles. Good conventions.

58. *www.dolfderoos.com.* Dolf DeRoos, New Zealand real estate.

59. *www.entrust.com.* Real estate investing with your IRA.

60. *www.fixerjay.com.* Jay Decima, author of *Fixin' Ugly Houses for Money.*

61. *www.flippinghomes.com.* Steve Cook's site. Wholesaling and rehabbing courses.

62. *www.johnreed.com.* Risky reading. Biased. Professional critic. Beware.

63. *www.landtrust.net.* Bill Gatten, home of PACTrust.

64. *www.lease2purchase.com.* Jeff Beaubien, lease/purchase made simple.
65. *www.midoh.com.* Mid-Ohio Securities, real estate investing with your IRA.
66. *www.money99.com.* John Adams, good basic information on real estate investing. Atlanta-based real estate newsletter is very good.
67. *www.mrlandlord.com.* Jeffrey Taylor, definitely for the property owner and property manager. Good value!
68. *www.notesmith.com.* Loan servicing software.
69. *www.realestatelink.net.* Many resources on creative real estate and a good discussion forum.
70. *www.realestatesuccess.com.* Scott Britton is a knowledgeable, down-to-earth investor/teacher.
71. *www.rehabwiz.com.* Kevin Myers, author of *Buy It, Fix It, Sell It: Profit!*
72. *www.realestatecoursereviews.com.* Go here to read Amazon-type reviews on some on the preceding gurus from real real estate investors.

You Want to Explore Commercial Real Estate Investing?

73. *www.ccim.com.* Commercial real estate investor Web site.
74. *www.housingfinance.com.* Web site for apartment financing.
75. *www.nrei.com.*
76. *www.vandema.com.* All about commercial real estate.

People Active in Real Estate: Industry Trade Groups

77. *www.nmhc.org.* The National Multi-Housing Unit Council represents the interests of the nation's larger and most

prominent apartment firms. NMHC conducts apartment-related research and encourages the exchange of strategic business information. Great free newsletter tells you where all the big money is going.

78. *www.namb.org.* National Association of Mortgage Brokers. Since mortgage brokers participate in more than 68 percent of home loan originations, home buyers' interests are also important to NAMB. Great place to start if you want to get into the business.

79. *www.a-e-a.org.* American Escrow Association. This industry trade group Web site has a great Q&A section that demystifies the escrow process.

80. *www.alta.org.* American Land Title Association (ALTA).

81. *www.arello.org.* National Organization of Real Estate Licensing Officials.

82. *www.boma.com.* Building Owners and Managers Association.

83. *www.fanniemae.com.*

84. *www.freddiemac.com.*

85. *www.hud.org.* Housing and Urban Development (HUD).

86. *www.infoville.com.* National Council of Exchangors. Great way to find a licensed 1031 exchange accommodator.

Nationwide Neighborhoods: Find Out What's Going on in Any Town: Demographics, Desirability Indexes, Crime Statistics, Schools, and How They Rank

87. *www.podunk.com.* If you don't know what is going on in an area, this is the place for just about any town in the country, no matter how small.

So You Want to Be a Landlord: Find Out the Rental Market

88. *www.realfacts.com.* An excellent resource to track multiunit vacancy rates nationwide.

89. *www.rhol.org.* Nearly anything related to the rental housing business.

90. *www.landlord.com.* Great resource for forms. Over one million members nationwide.

91. *www.mrlandlord.com.* Has links to landlord-tenant laws in all 50 states.

92. *www.aoausa.com.* Apartment Owners Association. An excellent resource. Has a tenant screening service for credit history, bounced checks, and previous evictions. Membership includes a very informative monthly newsletter.

93. *www.rentlaw.com.* One of the best multifaceted landlord resources I have seen. Highly recommended. Has landlord-tenant laws state by state and information on 1031 exchanges, section 8 vouchers, limited-liability companies (LLCs), sample lease agreements, and much more.

List Your Houses for Rent at Low to No Cost: Check Your Immediate Area for Best Results

94. *www.rentals.com.*

95. *www.forrent.com.*

96. *www.ezrentlist.com.*

97. *www.rent.com.*

98. *www.rentals.com.*

99. *www.westsiderentals.com.*

100. *www.craigslist.com.*

101. *www.rentreadyinc.com.*

102. *www.oodle.com.*

Know Thy Law: Legal Web Sites

103. *www.statelocalgov.net.* A great governmental resource that lists all state and local laws.

104. *www.brbpub.com.* Government public records online. Access U.S. government information online. Look up all state and federal laws.

105. *www.irs.gov.* Internal Revenue Service (IRS).

106. *www.legalwiz.com.* Bill Bronchick, informative attorney specializing in creative real estate. Highly recommended.

107. *www.legalzoom.com.* Great Web site that has legal information in all areas. Create your own living trust, limited-liability corporation, or corporation.

108. *www.nolopress.com.* Great free newsletters for whatever legal situation you are in.

Find a Home Inspection Company

109. *www.nahi.org.* National Association of Home Inspectors.

Meet with Other Investors: Find a Real Estate Investors Club in Your Town

110. *www.reica.com.* Real Estate Investment Clubs of America.

111. *www.reiclub.com.* National Real Estate Investment Clubs.

Talk Virtually to Other People Like You: Real Estate Chat Rooms

112. *www.creonline.* Informative discussions with a good following of "regulars." Good newsrooms and information regarding legal issues, financing, and mobile homes.

113. *www.dealmakerscafe.com.* Discussions on creative real estate hosted by Dealmaker. Lots of free articles.
114. *www.flippinghomes.com.* Discussions on wholesaling and rehabbing property hosted by Steve Cook.
115. *www.foreclosuretalk.com.* Discussions focused on PACTrust hosted by Bill Gatten.
116. *www.lease2purchase.com.* Discussions focused on lease/purchase hosted by Jeff Beauben.
117. *www.legalwiz.com.* Discussions on legal aspects of real estate hosted by Bill Bronchick.
118. *www.realestatelink.net.* Discussions on creative real estate.

Government Grants to Help You Buy Your First Residence

119. *www.hud.gov/local/local/ca/buying/prgrmscity.com.* Registry for all government grant programs.
120. *www.ncsha.org.* National Council of State Housing Agencies. Find out the government agency in your state that will provide financial assistance or maybe even a free down payment for your first home.

Miscellaneous

121. *www.car.org.* The California Association of Realtor's Web site is a very good source of raw economic data for state trends in housing affordability and housing strength in all California areas.
122. *www.dof.ca.org.* This State of California Department of Finance site offers very good demographic data. It is very detailed and will tell you where people are moving, population data, the kinds of jobs, and how much they make.

2

50 QUESTIONS TO ASK REAL ESTATE AGENTS AND PROPERTY MANAGERS

Real Estate Agents

1. What areas do you cover? How well do you know the growth patterns of the town?
2. How long have you been in the business?
3. How do you work with investors? Walk me through the process.
4. What types of properties do you specialize in?
5. Do you have any investments of your own?
6. What type of housing do you recommend for investors, single family, condos, multifamily? Why?
7. What kind of market are you experiencing? What kinds of markets have you experienced over the last five years? (Describe price changes, list price-to-sales-price ratios, inventory changes, etc.)

✗ 8. What kinds of industry and jobs are in the area? Where are they located? What are the best areas for rentals? Why?

9. Are there a lot of investors buying in the neighborhood? How many owner occupants will be living there?

10. Do you have a property manager that you would recommend?

11. What are the projected rents for my property? How did you come up with that?

Property Managers

12. What is the rental market like? For single family? For multi-family? What is the vacancy rate? What kinds of people rent single-family homes versus multiunits?

13. How long does a property remain vacant between tenants?

14. What are best areas for rentals?

15. What types of amenities will tenants pay extra for? Garage door openers? Enclosed yard? Pets?

16. What kinds of maintenance and other costs should I expect?

17. Is there rent control in your area? Do you see it coming?

18. What new developments are coming to your area?

19. How desirable is this housing tract to renters? Where do the renters work, and how far do they have to drive to work?

20. Are there a lot of other investors buying houses in the neighborhood?

Regarding Services

21. What areas do you cover? What do you charge? What fees should I expect? Is there an initial lease-up fee? If the tenant stays, is there a release fee?

22. Are you one of the biggest property management companies in town? Where do you rank in size?

23. Who pays for advertising, you or me?
24. What will you do if rent isn't paid on time?
25. How often do you do inspections? Do you drive by? Take photos?
26. Will you inspect property repairs after they are done? Do you charge an inspection fee?
27. How do you qualify tenants?
28. Do you verify previous landlords? Do you go back two or three?
29. How many pages in your rental agreement?
30. How often do I receive reports/statements from you? Would you give me an example?
31. Can you fax me the tenant's credit report and application?
32. What rental agreement do you use?
33. What do you do to keep up-to-date on landlord/tenant rights?
34. Have you ever had to evict anyone?
35. If you need an eviction, do you perform the eviction, or do you hire an eviction service?
36. How much is your late fee?
37. Do you offer the tenant any incentive for paying early?
38. Do you give the owner any late fees?
39. How do you handle repairs?
40. How many properties/units do you manage? How many are vacant?
41. Do you own any rentals?
42. Are you a full-time property manager? Do you do real estate sales too? Are you licensed?
43. How many people do you have working for you?
44. What happens when you go on vacation? Who handles the property management?
45. How do you market (advertise) your rentals?
46. Will you run a separate ad for my property, or do you just run one blanket ad for all your properties?
47. What is the vacancy rate on the properties you manage?

48. Who do you use for repairs? Do you have a team of handymen and contractors? Are they all licensed? How did you choose them? Do they charge market rates, or do you get a kickback from them?
49. Would you provide me with referrals—current owners and former owners you once worked with?
50. Do you have a real estate agent you would recommend?

INDEX

Commissioned income, 20
Compensating factors (for loans), 38
Condominiums, 16, 25
Consumer debt, 7, 82
Controlling transactions, 101–106
Cost of Funds Index (COFI), 52–53
Cost of money, 81
CPA (certified public accountant), 103
Creative financing, 116
Credit history, 32–36, 145
Credit reports, 20–22, 35
Credit scores, 32–35

Debt:
    documenting, 20–22
    responsible management of, 117
    tax deductions for interest on, 8–10
    types of, 7, 87 (*See also* Loans)
Debt-to-income ratios, 29–32
Demographic resources, 143–144
Depreciation, 118
Derivatives, 11
Down payment, 37, 74, 76
Duplexes, 16, 17, 25–26

Echo-boomer generation, 47, 48
Economic trends, 146
80/20 loans, 76–77
Eminent-domain laws, 2
Equifax, 20, 32, 35
Escrow fee, 98
Experian, 20, 32, 35
E.Z. doc loans, 69, 70

Fair Isaac Company (FICO), 32
Fannie Mae, 46, 90
Federal funds rate, 13–14
Federal Reserve, 13–14, 63, 95
Fee simple, 26
FICO (Fair Isaac Company), 32
FICO scores, 32–35
15-year fixed-rate loans, 50–51
Final closing statement (HUD-1), 106
Finding deals, 113–115
5 percent down loans, 11
5/25 hybrid loans, 58, 59
Fixed-interest-only loans, 11
Fixed-rate loans, 49–51, 67, 68
Flippers, 29
For Sale by Owner (FSBO) properties, 113
Foreclosures, 15, 35–36, 142
Forward commitment, 96
Fourplexes, 16, 17, 25–26
Freddie Mac, 46, 90

Free property profiles, 145
FSBO (For Sale by Owner) properties, 113

Gentrification, 121
Gift funds, 37
Ginnie Mae, 46
Government grants, 152
Granny flats, 27
Greenspan, Alan, 14
Gurus, 146–148

HELOC (*see* Home equity line of credit)
Home equity line of credit (HELOC), 53, 85–88
Home inspection companies, 151
Home ownership, 1–2
House prices, 48
HUD-1, 106
Hybrid loans/mortgages, 58–59, 64, 67

Immigration, 47, 48
Income:
    debt-to-income ratios, 29–32
    documenting, 19–20
    and stated income loans, 11, 22–23, 69–70
Indexes, financial, 52–53
Industry trade groups, 148–149
Inspections of property, 136
Installment debt, 87
Insurance, 131
Interest rates, 12–14
    annual percentage rate, 97–99
    caps on, 55–56
    on credit cards vs. mortgages, 82
    on credit lines, 86
    current, 10
    drivers of, 14
    locking in, 42–43, 95–97
    low (teaser) start rates, 56
    margin in determining, 54
    predicting, 12
    and refinancing, 80–81
    underlying financial indexes for, 52–53
    variability in, 63
Interest-only loans, 59–62
    adjustable-rate term of, 60–61
    best times to get, 67–68
    fixed-rate, 11
    100 percent loan-to-value ratio, 48–49
    overall amount of interest paid on, 61
    as "renting" a loan, 48
Intermediate-term fixed-rate (hybrid) loans, 67
Investment property:
    acquiring, 137–138
    as business, 139–140

About the Author

Since 1990, Steve Dexter has worked as a consultant advising people how to structure their loans to buy or refinance their properties. His degree in psychology earned at the University of Oklahoma in 1977 has helped him deal with people in all walks of life.

As president of National Capital Funding, he works every day helping people buy their first homes or investment properties. He specializes in aiding people acquire income-producing real estate through using the equity in their existing properties.

Steve and his wife, Susan, love to travel overseas to experience the many pleasures that the world has to offer.

He teaches real estate seminars at several community colleges in Southern California and coaches budding real estate agents and mortgage brokers.

Steve continues to mentor hundreds of real estate investors across the country. Many of his students have gone on to increase their cash flow and their wealth by using the concepts he teaches.

He writes a free bimonthly e-newsletter, "Economic News You Can Use." For a schedule of Steve's classes and a copy of his newsletter go to www.richdebt.com, call 1-888-993-9399, or write to Steve Dexter at 1278 Glenneyre, Suite 287, Laguna Beach, CA 92651.